D0069346

Margaret J. Barr, *Northwestern University*
EDITOR-IN-CHIEF

M. Lee Upcraft, *The Pennsylvania State University*
ASSOCIATE EDITOR

Enhancing the Multicultural Campus Environment: A Cultural Brokering Approach

Frances K. Stage
Indiana University

Kathleen Manning
University of Vermont

AUTHORS

Number 60, Winter 1992

JOSSEY-BASS PUBLISHERS
San Francisco

ENHANCING THE MULTICULTURAL CAMPUS ENVIRONMENT:
A CULTURAL BROKERING APPROACH
Frances K. Stage, Kathleen Manning (aus.)
New Directions for Student Services, no. 60
Margaret J. Barr, Editor-in-Chief
M. Lee Upcraft, Associate Editor

Microfilm copies of issues and articles are available in 16mm and 35mm, as well as microfiche in 105mm, through University Microfilms Inc., 300 North Zeeb Road, Ann Arbor, Michigan 48106.

LC 85-644751   ISSN 0164-7970   ISBN 1-55542-743-X

NEW DIRECTIONS FOR STUDENT SERVICES is part of The Jossey-Bass Higher and Adult Education Series and is published quarterly by Jossey-Bass Inc., Publishers, 350 Sansome Street, San Francisco, California 94104-1310 (publication number USPS 449-070). Second-class postage paid at San Francisco, California, and at additional mailing offices. POSTMASTER: Send address changes to New Directions for Student Services, Jossey-Bass Inc., Publishers, 350 Sansome Street, San Francisco, California 94104-1310.

SUBSCRIPTIONS for 1992 cost $45.00 for individuals and $60.00 for institutions, agencies, and libraries.

EDITORIAL CORRESPONDENCE should be sent to the Editor-in-Chief, Margaret J. Barr, 633 Clark Street, 2-219, Evanston, Illinois 60208-1103.

Cover photograph by Wernher Krutein/PHOTOVAULT © 1990.

Contents

8. A Vision of the Multicultural Campus 73

This chapter presents a vision of the multicultural campus for student affairs educators as we move toward a new millenium. The multicultural campus is focused on inclusion and openness.

AUTHORS' NOTES

The general college student body has evolved from a homogeneous, predominantly white population to one that is culturally, racially, and ethnically diverse. The higher education literature on this new multicultural population attempts to identify who the students are, how they differ from the "typical mainstream" student, and what can be done to enhance their college experiences. As a result, most student affairs professionals have become very adept at recognizing the obvious race-, gender-, and culture-based differences among college students. However, despite this wealth of everyday academic experience and the paper initiatives designed to help these students negotiate the college environment and develop to their full potential, deep-seated problems remain.

The findings of current research on achievement and retention of multicultural students are discouraging. Fewer African Americans, Latino Americans, and Native Americans attend college, success rates of those in college have not improved, and dreams of achieving educational equity remain unfulfilled. Additionally, incidents of racism reminiscent of the early 1960s have again flared on college campuses. No longer can one assume that the college environment is more enlightened than noneducational settings despite extensive implementation of strategies designed to improve the campus racial climate.

Suggestions for creating a multicultural campus environment typically place the burden for that development on those who are not part of the dominant culture. In essence, they are asked to integrate or assimilate themselves into the majority culture, to help one another, and to educate the mainstream. This approach assumes that students of color have similar interests in promoting racial and cultural diversity and acceptance. Additionally, in requiring identification of these students and overt actions to include them in campus life, the approach can lead to stereotyping of minority student groups. Furthermore, problems of invisible others (for example, the learning disabled, gays and lesbians, first-generation college attenders) are usually not addressed through this approach.

This book, *Enhancing the Multicultural Campus Environment: A Cultural Brokering Approach,* is not designed as a guide for identifying and describing these diverse populations and their development as college students. Other books, including recent issues in the New Directions for Student Services series, are excellent sources of that information. Rather, our central argument is that a more active approach must be taken by the higher education community, including those who are already working very hard to create multicultural campuses. We move forward from a descriptive perspective to suggest that more administrators and faculty need to become cultural brokers by learning to think contextually, span boundaries, ensure optimum performance, and take action.

The cultural broker model describes a way of practice used by many student affairs administrators on college campuses. It includes behavior that treats all students as individuals. The cultural broker model presents a vision of practice that can respond to the diversity of the 1990s and beyond. We provide examples of "cultural brokering" in college administrative practices that may be adopted more widely. This reflexive approach is defined as deliberate and thoughtful choices of action based on knowledge of cultural differences, expansion of personal experience to others' communities, education from a variety of perspectives, and advocacy for broadening opportunities. This individualized approach to working with students differs from the normatively defined administration practiced on many college campuses.

This book is designed to help college administrators and student affairs professionals who work directly with college students. Administrators make daily decisions that may serve the needs of some students but, because of traditional or mainstream cultural assumptions, may disenfranchise others. Faculty who have a variety of students in their classrooms should find this book useful in stimulating suggestions for flexibility in classroom practices. They might be interested in using this approach for the establishment of practice (for example, method of teaching) and testing (for example, writing culture-sensitive exams). Additionally, those who currently practice "cultural brokering" may find the model useful in refining their skills and in passing their expertise along to others.

Finally, this book is designed for those enrolled in student affairs preparation programs. Many graduate students will become new administrators in complex campus systems serving diverse student populations. For them, the perspectives and suggestions within the book should provide valuable insights about the creation and maintenance of multicultural campuses.

In attempting to put the concepts of the cultural broker model in writing, we struggled with word choice. We envision a campus climate in which reflexive administration, advising, and policy-making have a positive impact on all students, including ethnic and cultural minorities, students with disabilities, international students, first-generation attenders, gay, lesbian, and bisexual students, and returning students. In this volume, because of practical limitations, we write primarily about ethnic minorities. However, we envision the model as a means for empowering and freeing all students, including the dominant majority on campus. In an effort to be as inclusive as possible, we use the terms *diverse students* and *persons of color* interchangeably.

The following terms also appear throughout this volume. We present their definitions so that our meanings are clear to the reader.

1. *Culturally pluralistic:* a campus that recognizes a broad diversity of cultures and that does not pressure its students or staff to conform or assimilate to the dominant culture
2. *Dominant* or *majority culture:* the culture whose values predominate pervasively on campus, ranging from administrative decision making to architectural style
3. *Monocultural campus:* a campus that retains and expects traditions, styles, and ways of behaving characteristic of only one culture
4. *Multicultural campus:* a campus that recognizes and values the broad array of cultures characteristic of its students, staff, and faculty
5. *Multicultural students:* racial or ethnic minorities, women, and any other students who might feel disempowered by policies and practices of the predominant Eurocentric culture on many college campuses
6. *New perspectives:* inclusive and sensitive administrative practices resulting from an expanded understanding of a variety of cultures

Chapter One discusses situations on campus that preclude many colleges and universities from being described as multicultural. Reasons why many current strategies are not adequate for the task of creating a multicultural campus are also discussed. In Chapter Two, the cultural broker model is presented along with a general description of its application on campus. Chapters Three through Seven focus on specific areas of student services: administration, academics, students, residence halls, and the cocurriculum. Within each chapter, several important current issues in student affairs are discussed in light of the cultural broker model. Clear examples of implementation of the cultural broker approach are provided. Finally, Chapter Eight provides sources of additional reading and reconsiders issues presented in Chapter One with a vision of the future multicultural campus environment.

FRANCES K. STAGE *is associate professor of higher education and student affairs at Indiana University, Bloomington. Her work includes refereed articles, book chapters, and edited works on college students. She is an author of* Diverse Methods for Research and Assessment of College Students. *She has served on the editorial boards of* American College Personnel Association, Journal of College Student Development, *and* Review of Higher Education *and has received research awards from the Association for the Study of Higher Education and from Indiana University.*

KATHLEEN MANNING *is assistant professor of higher education and student affairs at the University of Vermont, Burlington. She has served as assistant dean of students at Emerson College, director of student activities at Curry College, and executive assistant to student life at Trenton State College. Her research and scholarly writing concern campus cultures, organizational development, multiculturalism, and qualitative research methodology applied to higher education. She is an author of* Diverse Methods for Research and Assessment of College Students.

Several vignettes depicting cultural conflicts that arise in various arenas of campus life are presented along with a brief description of the diversity of today's college student population and a discussion of program planning, teaching, and advising strategies currently employed on campus. Finally, the argument is made that these strategies are not equal to the task of creating a multicultural campus.

The Multicultural Campus

Vignette One

Professor Brown teaches a class of approximately 150 undergraduates, most of whom are first-year students and sophomores taking the course to fulfill general distribution requirements. Other students plan to earn the professional degree that Brown's department grants. Brown prides himself on his teaching; he enjoys trying innovative techniques that challenge students and stimulate learning. He teaches the largest class on campus, yet it is one of the most popular.

One of Brown's students approaches him toward the end of the semester. Carmen, a student athlete, was recruited from a South American country. She has been having trouble in the class and would like a chance to do some extra-credit work. Carmen's participation in the small discussion section for the class has been uneven. She sometimes misses class, but when she is there, she participates even though her English is imperfect. Her essay answers on quizzes frequently do not make sense, and her scores tend to be low.

Brown considers her request and decides against granting any special favors to a particular student. The grading methods have been clearly spelled out ahead of time and to alter them for one student would be unfair. Besides, allowing individuals to do extra credit to make up for poor performance may result in a lowering of standards for the whole class.

Vignette Two

For four years, Student Activities Director Williams has advised the campus student body officers and the student senate. He prides himself on the fact that student government is truly self-government. He restricts his activities to advising and does not attempt to influence decisions of the officers. In fact, he is so careful to present the logic of alternative perspectives that, on most issues, students do not know where he stands.

Each year the student senate is faced with the task of allocating funds to various campus interest groups. Officers from these groups must make presentations of their proposed budgets to the senate. After questioning the club officers regarding their plans for spending, the senate votes on allocation of the money.

For the past two years, the campus Gay, Lesbian, and Bisexual Alliance has made a request for organizational funding for both social and educational activities. Both years, after much heated discussion, the request has been rejected. Arguments proffered by students against the funding center on the claims that the organization is for a specialized group of people, it does not meet the needs of the general campus population, and it seeks to corrupt "innocent" others. The alliance counters that they are primarily an educational and a social group and do nothing to advocate specific sexual activities.

Williams disagrees with the senate's decision but does not want to violate his own standards of professional performance. He recognizes a basic unfairness in the student senate decision. In his advice to campus leaders, he reminds them of other clubs that regularly receive funding but that do not meet the needs of the general student population. Aside from such advice, Williams decides that any other efforts may be viewed as an intrusion on the autonomy of the student governance system. He attributes the students' decision to the increasing conservatism of college students in general and thinks that the decision probably reflects the wishes of the student majority.

Vignette Three

Residence Life Director Waters is the head of a large residence system at a midwestern university. Since assuming the director's position several years ago, Waters has made several changes that address the development of the whole student rather than simply the living needs of the student. She is particularly proud of the efforts directed at multicultural awareness, an issue sometimes neglected on large campuses. Cultural differences, however, continue to be a problem.

She was contacted one morning by the parent of a first-year student. The parent, a state legislator, was trying to use political influence to get a new roommate for his son, Rob. The university assigns roommates in a random fashion, and Rob's roommate is African American. The parent was incredulous that Waters actually expected whites and blacks to live together and vowed to go as high as possible in order to get the assignment changed.

A call to the head resident confirmed that there had been problems. The black roommate, Dave, thought he had heard a racist remark from Rob's parents on the day that he moved in. Rob has not spoken to Dave, and, frequently, when Dave returns to his room, a group of Rob's friends is there and seems to be staring at him. Several efforts by hall staff to get them to communicate have been unsuccessful. Dave has begun to feel quite uncomfortable and has told his resident adviser that he would like a new roommate.

Waters considers the possible negative effects of allowing this change: (1) It would reinforce the ethnocentrism of Rob, the white student involved. (2) Both students would miss the opportunity to live and learn from someone culturally different from themselves. And (3) the implication of the move would be that the residence life department does not really stand firm in its multicultural efforts. Waters decides against a change of roommates.

The scenarios presented above are not unlike the dilemmas facing those who work with students on today's changing college campuses. The administrators and faculty described above, like many of us, were well meaning and conscientious. They had obviously put thought into their policies and decision making. Their judgments seemed to demonstrate the exercise of sound professional values and considered ethical choice. However, the lines of reasoning given for the decisions made in these instances had a similar ring of rigidity in terms of "doing what is in the best interest" of the majority of students. What was originally intended to be equal treatment was not equal in most cases. With each of these decisions, the multicultural student suffered.

In the first vignette, Professor Brown made several assumptions about Carmen that resulted in the rejection of her request. He chose not to view her approach as a general entreaty for help. He dealt only with the request for extra-credit assignments. He assumed that timed and written exams and quizzes were adequate ways to test whether Carmen had learned the course material. He did not consider any alternative means of testing, despite his observations of her uneven language performance. Finally, he assumed that unless he treated all students in exactly the same manner, he was being unfair. In short, he viewed her as one of many students in a large class rather than as an athlete who speaks English as a second language and also happens to be in his class. Additionally, it seems the administration that recruited Carmen for her athletic abilities does nothing to "level the playing field" in the classroom.

In the second vignette, Student Activities Director Williams presumed that the elected student body was representative of and voted according to the best interests of the student population as a whole. However, frequently, the elected student government is a cadre of privileged students who, in terms of demographics, social status, and motivations, are representative of only a small proportion of the actual student body. Williams also assumed that the student senate had the education and maturity to deal with difficult legal decisions. Finally, he assumed that he could perform his job best by assuming a laissez-faire philosophy rather than by actively educating the students with whom he worked. A better solution to this issue might have involved switching from majority rule to an understanding of all of the constituencies of student government.

Finally, in the third vignette, Residence Life Director Waters also made several assumptions that could possibly harm Dave, the African American student. By implication, she assumed that it was the responsibility of Dave and other multicultural students to educate majority culture students about diversity. Additionally, she assumed that by living together, the two students would grow to appreciate one another. She expected that mere enforcement of rules would bring about change in the students involved. Finally, she seemed to assume that maintaining the reputation of the residence life department, as an organization dedicated to pluralistic living environments, was of utmost importance in this situation. In her consideration of courses of action, she did not appear to take the perspective of the multicultural student who must face the challenges of a new, predominantly white campus environment and then return "home" to a hostile roommate.

Perhaps if the administrators and faculty described above had viewed their respective dilemmas from an alternative perspective, the multicultural students involved could have been empowered in the situations rather than rejected. The purpose of this chapter is to present the multicultural campus as it currently exists, as an elusive and complex entity. We begin with a brief description of the diversity of today's college student population. We then discuss strategies of program planning, teaching, and advising that are currently employed on many campuses and the reasons why these strategies are not equal to the task before us. Finally, we conclude with the assertion that new, more inclusive perspectives for administrators are needed, perspectives that can help create a truly multicultural campus environment.

The Multicultural Campus Today

The process of educating the college student has become increasingly complex. As college campuses admit more diverse clientele, changes in policies and procedures must be made. As we saw in the above vignettes, practices and decision making that may be adequate for the majority of students often work to disenfranchise those who are not a part of the majority culture.

Recently, college administrators and faculty have increasingly demonstrated awareness of and concern for multicultural college students. Throughout the 1970s, expansion of civil rights, the women's movement, increased sensitivity to cultural heterogeneity, open-door policies, and expanded financial aid programs provided broader access to higher education for historically disenfranchised American students. In twenty years, the general college student body in the United States has changed from a homogeneous, male, predominantly white population to one that is increasingly becoming culturally, racially, and ethnically mixed (American Association of State Colleges and Universities, 1988; Estrada, 1988; Fenske and Hughes, 1989; Commission on Minority Participation in Education and American Life, 1988; Smith, 1989). Probably the University of Hawaii at Manoa represents a futuristic view of the college campus. There, the white students, *haoles,* represent less than 30 percent of the campus population. In addition to African American, Latino American, Native American, and international students, there is a diverse population of Pacific Islander Americans and Asian Americans, the most populous of whom are the Chamorros, the Chinese, the native Hawaiians, the Hmong, the Japanese, the Koreans, the Micronesians, the Filipinos, the Samoans, the Tongans, and the Vietnamese (Palafox and Warren, 1980).

The higher education literature on multicultural populations attempts to identify today's college students (Taylor, 1986), show that there is no longer a "typical mainstream" student (Cross, 1985), and inform us of ways to enhance all students' college experiences (Blake, 1985; Manning, 1988; Manning and Coleman-Boatwright, 1991; Pounds, 1987; Richardson, Simmons, and de los Santos, 1987; Taylor, 1986). To be sure, as educators we have become very good at recognizing the obvious racial, gender, and ethnic differences among college students. And we are slowly making progress at understanding the relationships between multicultural students' experiences and success in college (Stage, 1990). However, despite this wealth of "academic experience" and the paper initiatives designed to help these students negotiate the college environment and develop to their full potential, deep-seated problems remain.

The most current research on achievement and retention of multicultural students has produced discouraging findings. Fewer African Americans, Latino Americans, and Native Americans attend college, success rates of those in college have not improved, and dreams of achieving educational equity remain unfulfilled (American Association of State Colleges and Universities, 1988; Fields, 1988; Olivas, 1986; Commission on Minority Participation in Education and American Life, 1988; Richardson, Simmons, and de los Santos, 1987; Thiers, 1987; Wilson and Carter, 1988). Studies have shown that the educational climate at predominantly white institutions of higher education operates to thwart the academic success of most multicultural students (Fleming, 1984; Hughes, 1987; Munoz, 1986; Olivas, 1986). Additionally, incidents of racism reminiscent of the early 1960s have plagued college campuses (Collison, 1987; Steele, 1989). No longer can one assume that the college environment is more enlightened than noneducational settings, despite the work of student affairs personnel and extensive implementation of strategies designed to improve the campus racial climate.

The late 1980s saw the emergence of alarmingly popular tomes decrying the movement of higher education toward cultural pluralism (Bloom, 1987; Hirsch, 1987). These emergent notions of higher education included moribund visions of a higher education enterprise bound by conventional wisdoms of the past (for an excellent counterargument to Bloom and Hirsch, see Simonson and Walker, 1988). The Bloom and Hirsch higher education system would have transmission of knowledge rather than discourse and mutual construction of knowledge as its highest goal. Giroux (1988a) decries these visions as plans to foster and reinforce traditional power and privilege. In speaking of change on college campuses in a speech to the American College Personnel Association, former congresswoman Shirley

Chisholm (1991) stated that "tradition is no longer the answer to the problems we are grappling with today" and "traditions on the campus can no longer be carried out when traditions are no longer appropriate to the situation."

Charges abound that colleges and universities seeking to foster pluralistic campuses are trying to create "politically correct" environments (Adler and others, 1990; DePalma, 1991; Emerson, 1991). Given the sorry state of pluralism on college campuses, Cheatham (1991a, 1991b) chastises the higher education enterprise for the lack of results. "What is evident is that after two recent decades of bold, new societal efforts for providing equity in U.S. higher education the retention and graduation results are uneven and unenviable" (1991b, p. 33). He also decries the lack of leadership aimed toward changes in the near future. "Instead of providing leadership in the resolution of one of our major social problems [racism], collegiate institutions essentially have passively reflected the values and attitudes of the society at large" (1991a, p. 14).

It is clear that in the remainder of this decade the achievement of a multicultural campus, a goal that has eluded most colleges to now, will continue to be a key task. One way of approaching this issue is to critically examine current attempts to establish multicultural campus environments.

Why Current Strategies Are Flawed

College administrators are gradually becoming aware that traditional approaches to program planning, teaching, and advising are based on theories derived from research on middle- and upper-class, predominantly Eurocentric student populations (Stage, 1989a). This research and the resultant approaches have neither met the needs of nor even been particularly applicable to students who are different from those on whom the research was based (McEwen, Roper, Bryant, and Langa, 1990).

This early recognition of the limited applicability of traditional theories and approaches led to a decade of "armchair" advice for improving campus racial climates and incorporating multicultural students into the mainstream. Typically, these recommendations included (1) bringing members of a particular group together during orientations and focusing on their special needs, (2) working closely with the parents of multicultural students and with faculty and administrators to build a network of support that connects the campus support group with the family, (3) identifying multicultural faculty and administrators, introducing them to students, and asking them to serve as advisers and mentors, (4) encouraging students in racial and ethnic minority groups to socialize with one another and form support networks and clubs, and (5) encouraging students in these groups to participate in campus activities with predominantly mainstream students.

Administrators are beginning to realize that these relatively "piecemeal efforts" and "special programs" are not the answer to what is a more complex and deeply rooted problem (Jaschik, 1988). In making suggestions for creating pluralistic campus environments, Richard C. Richardson, Jr., states that "colleges that are trying to attract more minority students and faculty members had thought of the various approaches as a sort of Chinese menu— you can take one idea from this column and another from that. . . . To succeed, colleges must instead create a seamless fabric of efforts, extending over the entire institution" (Jaschik, 1988, p. 31).

The reasons that these piecemeal strategies may be helpful but not adequate to the task of creating a multicultural college environment are not immediately obvious. Problems with the efforts can be described in terms of several central issues: (1) assuming that diverse students must change, (2) making multicultural students, faculty, and administrators already in the institution responsible for socializing new multicultural students, (3) encouraging multicultural students to adapt to the dominant culture, (4) helping only "identifiable" multicultural students, (5) failing to provide equitable educational opportunities to all students admitted to the institution, and (6) failing to educate those of the dominant culture about their multicultural colleagues.

The motives behind the strategies are good, but in themselves they constitute a far from adequate response to multicultural demands. The above six issues define typical campus recommendations that appear at first blush to be idealistically sound but have fallen short of achieving multicultural campus environments.

First, some strategies assume that it is the responsibility of multicultural students to adjust and become socialized into a college environment that may be very different from their past educational experiences and their home communities. These adjustments may be as simple as adapting to the type of social events offered on campus, or as complex as adapting to expectations in classroom behaviors and assignments that differ from what the student currently knows. At the same time, diverse students struggle with all of the difficulties and stresses that all students confront as they make the transition into college study (Hughes, 1987).

Under the assumption that "mainstreaming" of multicultural students is the best way for all of them to adjust to college life, these students often are placed with white students in residence halls and encouraged to go out of their way to join dominant college organizations and to socialize with those outside of their own cultural or ethnic groups. These multicultural students thus face a double adjustment. While they are adjusting to college learning demands, trying to negotiate an unfamiliar campus, and learning to take care of themselves without their parents, they must also adapt to a new campus culture in other realms of their lives.

Second, often primary responsibility is placed on multicultural group members who are already part of the institution to play a proactive role in the socializing process. This strategy involves activities such as providing African American students with African American advisers, creating peer mentoring programs for diverse students, and hosting special orientations for new Latino American students to meet Latinos already on campus. These activities help to build the necessary supportive environment for diverse students. However, there simply are not enough diverse administrators, faculty, and students to meet the need. Additionally, in this strategy those who are part of the dominant culture play a passive role and do not share responsibility for creating a hospitable environment for all students. Multicultural individuals are asked to take responsibility for representing "their cultures" and mentoring the large numbers of students of color. Meanwhile, they also are attempting to make their way within an institution dominated by the symbols and practices of another culture.

Third, by encouraging multicultural students to join organizations predominantly composed of white students, the assumption is made that the multicultural student shares the interests of the dominant culture student. Rather than recognize the culturally determined variety of students' interests, organizations are based on a dominant culture model to which diverse students must adapt. This practice of ignoring the need for organizations dealing specifically with diverse students' interests embodies the belief that their cultures are inferior to the dominant culture. It implies that they should adapt to a culture different from their own, one more valued within the institution. Multicultural students are deprived of a celebration and affirmation of their respective cultures. And all students are thereby deprived of the opportunity to learn about a variety of cultures.

Fourth, in order to be aided by most of these strategies, diverse students must be identified and encouraged to participate actively. There are diverse students who work to assimilate themselves into the dominant campus culture. These students may struggle with the issue of whether or not to identify themselves as "different" from other students. They resist outreach or support and are thus unlikely to receive the services to which they are entitled. In addition to any of these targeted approaches, there is a need for an attitude of acceptance where the multicultural student is not set apart as an anomaly but celebrated as a full member of a pluralistic society.

Fifth, as higher education exists today, the majority of institutions fail in their obligation to provide equitable educational opportunities to all students admitted. Statistics comparing college success rates of white students with those of Native Americans, African Americans, Latinos, and Asian Americans clearly demonstrate this failure (American Association of State Colleges and Universities, 1988; Fields, 1988; Olivas, 1986; Commission on Minority Participation in Education and American Life, 1988; Richardson, Simmons, and de los Santos, 1987; Thiers, 1987; Wilson and Carter, 1988). For students of the dominant culture, the campus is more readily negotiable. The decisions, activities, and policies of the administration, in effect, serve the dominant culture student. Those of diverse cultures are left to serve one another. If we accept, even recruit, students into the campus community, we have a legal and moral obligation to fulfill the promise of an equitable education.

Finally, interventions implemented on most college campuses have not required any fundamental change in the dominant campus culture. This intransigence precludes examination of the underlying assumptions that create the barriers to free expression of cultural differences. Limited demands are made of those people in the mainstream to learn about others' cultures. An ethnocentric attitude remains in any administrative action that envisions and plans interventions only from the perspective of the dominant culture. The ultimate implication of this approach is "be like us, think like us, and act like us" rather than a mutual adjustment to the wide diversity of possibilities in life.

Success on some campuses depends on students' ability to assimilate their personal and public styles into the dominant culture. Fortunately, some multicultural students are unwilling or unable to make the shift. However, the pattern of response to such an incongruent environment might be to partially or totally disengage in some way from the institution (Fleming, 1984). Disengagement may be a refusal to participate in any but similar culture events such as African American student-sponsored activities. Other students may participate only in classes and socialize entirely off campus. Still others, many others, discouraged and alienated, leave the institution. Few campuses have reached the point where students of color can successfully integrate without compromising their cultural heritages. The tragedy is that the culture of the student who elects to assimilate is denied as well as that of the student who disengages. One student may shed his or her culture. Another student may mask the culture and let it show only when she or he is sure that it is shared by others present. A third student gradually disengages and then drops out of college. These students are robbed of the freedom to be themselves. This response narrows the cultural diversity possible within the college community, and cultures that vary from the dominant one disappear or go "underground." Students of the dominant culture learn little from their "exposure" to other cultures. All students lose the freedom to engage totally in the educational process.

The Need for New Perspectives

The average college professor or administrator probably has developed methods or "theories of action" for working with diversity issues on today's campus. Although experience shows that student affairs administrators need to further modify their behaviors, research demonstrates that theories of action are difficult to change and that people generally do not notice evidence that refutes their own personal theories. One tends to recognize only those experiences that reinforce one's theory of action (Argyris, 1976). Thus, the process of attempting to modify the ways in which one makes decisions and sets policy may be difficult. As administrators then, we must continually seek feedback from others as to how our actions affect them as individuals.

In this chapter, we have presented evidence that some of the most frequently employed strategies for creating a multicultural campus are not working. In the remainder of the book, we present a model for creating a multicultural campus. It moves beyond mere recognition of others as distinct from those of the dominant culture. Ideally, the model's "seamless fabric of efforts" will result in a campus that fosters multiple ways of being. The ultimate goal is for action that moves us toward diverse others so that all on the multicultural campus will be changed for the better.

It is clear that as we move toward the next millennium, college administrators must broaden their views of what it takes to create a multicultural campus environment. In writing of similar issues, Giroux (1988a) and Tierney (1991) used the phrase "border-crossers." We borrow it to describe the multicultural student on today's typical college campus. These students move back and forth across physical and cultural borders in their negotiation of the campus environment. In our vision of the campus of the future, these borders still exist, but they are less treacherous and more readily traversed. Additionally, they are crossed not just by multicultural students but by administrators, faculty, and students of all cultures.

The cultural broker model, incorporating the steps of learning to think contextually, spanning boundaries, ensuring optimum performance, and taking action, is explained in detail. Examples are offered for further understanding of the goals of multiculturalism.

The Cultural Broker: A Role for Student Affairs Educators

This chapter illustrates the cultural broker model and explores the process of making college campuses more inclusive. The model, framed in the context of a pluralistic American society, describes changes in administrative and educational practice necessary for success within present-day campus settings (Manning and Stage, 1987). The model is based on the work of Paulo Freire (1970, 1973, 1985), Jacqueline Fleming (1984), Anthony Giddens (1979, 1984), and Shirley Brice Heath (1983). In particular, Heath's concept of the educator as "cultural broker" serves as the centerpiece of the cultural broker model.

Assumptions of the Cultural Broker Model

The first assumption of the cultural broker model is that campuses, similar to other American social institutions, were built on monocultural, specifically Eurocentric, cultural norms (Colon, 1991; Fellows, 1972; J. Jones, 1988; Katz, 1989; Schaef, 1985). On the basis of Eurocentric traditions, especially the emphasis on logic and the scientific method, scholars and researchers have made substantial advancements in terms of scientific discoveries, disease control, and technological progress, to name only a few areas. But similar to any one worldview or perspective, the Eurocentric model has both strengths and weaknesses. A weakness of any monocultural perspective (Eurocentric or otherwise) is its inflexibility and failure to consider other cultural traditions and viewpoints. In this volume, we do not advocate pursuit of the impossible and ill-conceived task of dismantling the Eurocentric perspective on campuses. Rather, we describe a campus perspective that is more inclusive of various points of view and ways of being. The goal, through the cultural broker model, is to create a new educational system that empowers campus participants by recognizing and emphasizing the strengths of various cultural systems while also recognizing their weaknesses (D. W. Sue and D. Sue, 1990). Monoculturalism is an environment or situation where one culture is either consciously or unconsciously viewed as superior and is, therefore, the *only* culture reflected in the organizational structure and public practices of the institution (Katz, 1989). Colleges and universities, if they are to survive in an increasingly ethnically and culturally diverse American society, *can* and *must* change from a monoculturalist to multiculturalist perspective.

A second assumption of the cultural broker model is that student affairs educators, influential on campus, fulfill pivotal roles in moving campuses toward multiculturalism (Ebbers and Henry, 1990). The task ahead for student affairs educators is to shape a campus environment that is truly multicultural.

A third assumption of the model is that the transformation from monoculturalism to multiculturalism requires a fundamental alteration in the way that business is conducted on campus (Jaschik, 1987). The challenge for student affairs educators is to encourage cultural pluralism without cultural relativism, that is, believing that *everything* about a culture is of value regardless of the context. Rather than embracing "witless relativism" (Geertz, 1986), a pluralistic campus incorporates practices that empower students of all cultures to succeed and develop to their full potential.

The Cultural Broker Model

The cultural broker model describes a method of operation that empowers all students to become involved in the campus community (Manning and Stage, 1987). The primary emphasis of this effort is organizational and systemic change by student affairs educators, faculty, students (majority students as well as students of color), and other campus participants. The components of the model—learn to think contextually, span boundaries, ensure optimal performance, and take action—reflect responsiveness to *all* persons regardless of race, ethnicity, or culture. A multicultural campus, the goal of the cultural broker model, is achieved by recognizing and changing the organizational barriers that stand in the way of inclusion. Colleges need to create a "seamless fabric of efforts," extending over the entire institution in order to achieve multiculturalism.

Learn to Think Contextually. Current efforts in student affairs toward cultural diversity focus on recognizing, appreciating, and celebrating differences. People learn the habits and traditions of various cultures in order to share and celebrate differences and similarities. The complete achievement of a multicultural environment is not reached, however, through this celebration of differences approach as white students learn about the "other" in order to better succeed in a pluralistic society. White, primarily middle-class students learn the cultural histories of African Americans, Latino Americans, Asian Americans, and Native Americans in an effort to understand and work productively with people of various cultures. For students of color, the process of learning the ways of the "other" predates current cultural diversity efforts. Regardless of ethnicity or culture, they must learn the ways of the dominant culture (Katz, 1985, 1989) in order to be successful in American society. In response they have developed communities in which they exercise cultural traditions, friends with whom they speak their first language or cultural vernacular, and safe places where they can reveal certain opinions. They have learned to survive in situations where they experience disdain for their cultural nuances, language, and traditions (Jones, Terrell, and Duggar, 1991).

People who do not hold to dominant culture norms learn to recognize contexts where various types of knowledge and behavior are acceptable or unacceptable. They learn to "switch" or use a variety of cultural and personal styles depending on the context (Fellows, 1972). This switching is referred to by an assortment of derogatory terms: girl talk, fag talk. The student affairs educator in a culturally diverse setting must also learn to think and act contextually. In a college setting, this means understanding not only the dominant culture reflected in formal campus structures and practices but also all of the culturally diverse meanings and knowledge *within* the institution.

For administrators and faculty who, regardless of their race and gender, have only been exposed to the dominant culture, the responsibility to think contextually is formidable. The dominant culture is so obvious and pervasive in American society that those who incorporate its values and practices can remain virtually unaware of other cultural systems and still obtain a level of success and achievement as measured by the dominant culture. The cultural lens adopted throughout the individual's history and experiences becomes a generalized style and way to view the world: "People of all races, creeds and colors tend to view the world about them through their own eyes—through the lenses of their own culture" (Fellows, 1972, p. 10). This perspective, so much a part of that person, becomes an assumed reality rather than one of many ways to view the world. The increased numbers of diverse students on campus means that this time-honored approach may no longer guarantee success for present and future student affairs educators.

The task of learning to think contextually starts with an examination of one's underlying cultural assumptions. Student affairs educators who are cultural brokers examine their assumptions and become more aware of their beliefs and dialogue with others about those assumptions. This soul-searching process entails examination of a culture, including one's own, from a critical perspective, whereby strengths and weaknesses are recognized and made explicit (D. W. Sue and D. Sue, 1990). This awareness then builds to a realization that administrative actions and educational practices are not objective but rather reflect cultural backgrounds and assumptions. This awareness of the underlying beliefs of practice is called *reflexivity* (Giddens, 1984). It is a process of "stepping outside" of one's cultural heritage in order to gain a fuller understanding of how that perspective is only one of many on which actions can be based.

This recognition of multiple cultural systems challenges the practice of privileging one system over another. The goal is not to assume a relative perspective where *all* perspectives are haphazardly expressed. Rather, oppressive techniques that privilege one cultural system over others are recognized and abolished. In this way, knowledge can be expanded and diversified, thereby enhancing creativity and critical thinking.

By thinking contextually, in other words, within the boundaries of other cultures, student affairs educators as cultural brokers abandon their sole reliance on Eurocentrism (Katz, 1989), including its rigid dualism (for example, right and wrong), hierarchies of excellence (for example, good, better, best), and sanctioned ways of measuring intelligence (for example, standardized tests). This reliance is incompatible with the goals of multiculturalism. A multicultural rather than monocultural approach respects all talents as having value within the academic community (Astin, 1982; Blake, 1985). *All* students are viewed as having valuable cultural traditions, and these are reflected in the structural hierarchy and organization of the college or university. Student affairs educators actively work to create opportunities that open the campus up to an expression of these talents and perspectives.

Span Boundaries. Dialogue is a meaningful means in multicultural environments of spanning diverse campus cultures. A dialogical approach means that the student affairs educator seeks to understand what the student already knows when he or she arrives on campus rather than expecting the student to assimilate to the dominant culture (Heath, 1983). The culturally based knowledge involves assumptions about community living, time and space, language, traditions, and celebrations (Atkinson, Morten, and Sue, 1989; D. W. Sue and D. Sue, 1990). Student affairs educators who seek to span cultural boundaries view the student as "a unique individual while, at the same time, taking into consideration his or her common experiences as a human being (i.e., developmental challenges that face all people), as well as the specific experiences that come from the client's particular cultural background" (Lee and Richardson, 1991, p. 5). During dialogue, the student affairs educator does not privilege his or her own cultural knowledge above the student's but rather engages in honest and personally revealing cultural interaction (Freire, 1970). This stance means that the student affairs educator purposely loses objectivity as he or she relates to a student and becomes personally involved in an effort to gain knowledge intimately related to who that student is as a culturally defined person.

If student affairs educators fail to consider multicultural students as people with unique perspectives based on cultural knowledge, those students are only partially drawn into the college experience. Learning is not integrated with their past experiences and ways of being because they are treated as entities whose parts can be separated from the whole. When the dominant culture is presented to them as privileged over their own cultures, only the parts of them that correspond to the dominant culture are congruent with the learning process. A significant cultural dimension of their personas is ignored or denied in the context of campus life and academic endeavors. Under such circumstances, it is no surprise that students reject educational systems (for example, through attrition, protests, and disengagement) that do not respond to their cultural backgrounds (Fleming, 1984; Jackson, 1991). The difficulties of these circumstances are faced by multicultural students as well as by all students who have to deny parts of themselves and their backgrounds to adapt to campus life. These difficulties occur whether student affairs educators privilege the dominant culture or stereotype by assuming that the students have automatic allegiance to their respective cultures. "Beware of falling into the trap of easy stereotyping. Even people with good intentions stereotype—but the effects are still destructive. . . . Specific individuals have qualities and attributes outside of the parameters of our generalizations" (Davenport and Yurich, 1991, p. 66).

Heath (1983) suggests that educators critically view both the institutional culture and the students' individual cultures as they adopt their role as cultural brokers. Through this role they, as culturally informed educators, mediate and negotiate the boundaries of cultures. This brokering is not a matter of transmitting the dominant cultural *into* waiting students. Rather, cultural brokers work to understand and meet the students on their own cultural terms. The educators think contextually (that is, relate to the students on their cultural terrain by acquiring cultural knowledge and practicing dialogue) and use that ability to build bridges between all of the various cultures on campus. The practice of boundary spanning means trusting that students can learn using their own structures of knowledge rather than only using campus-sanctioned approaches. In environments where the "right way" to study, learn, and compete is clearly articulated, this trust represents a major change in administrative practice and academic procedure.

Freire's (1970) work concerning critical pedagogy provides a foundation for adopting knowledge, attitudes, and actions that are helpful to performance of the cultural broker role. The cultural broker empowers students through honest dialogue about the assumptions of administrative practice in relation to cultural differences and similarities. Administrative decisions are not habitually made according to the dominant perspective or without knowledge of cultural differences. Administrative practice is a medley of conscious acts that influences students' lives. The administrator evaluates the potential results of any action in terms of their effects on a diversity of students.

The use of administrative practice to span cultural boundaries involves asking oneself difficult questions. Are the interventions based *only* on one's own experiences? Or was information sought on the opinions and experiences of groups who comprise culturally distinct campus populations? Does the knowledge taught include students' background knowledge? Are the experiences from the histories and traditions of all students affirmed and respected in the college environment? Do programs and services of campus life represent aspects of various life-styles and ways of learning? Some campuses can answer yes to many of these questions, largely because of the efforts of student affairs staff. All campuses can do more to take leadership roles in considering multiple viewpoints, developing their cultural brokering skills, and encouraging others to do the same.

Ensure Optimal Performance. All students, whether of dominant or nondominant cultural backgrounds, have varying skills and approaches to learning and living within campus environments (Astin, 1989). Unfortunately, students of color, who have been historically denied full inclusion in higher education (Botstein, 1991; Cook and Helms, 1991; Hayes, 1985), have skills and ways of living that are not equally reflected in the campus environment.

College practices predominantly reflect the heritage and traditions of Eurocentric culture, with limited overt characteristics of other traditions (Botstein, 1991). For example, architecture may reflect the style of the region in which it is located: Spanish in California, Colonial in New England. But, in general, the historical and traditional style of collegiate architecture follows the English Oxbridge model of collegiate Gothic. Whether one is in Harvard Yard or Indiana University's historic Crescent Quadrangle, the Oxbridge influence is clearly evident. These traditional collegiate environments are familiar to those of the dominant culture who have been raised with traditional images of how a college "is supposed to look." Similarly, modes of teaching, food served in cafeterias, and styles of living match middle-class backgrounds, suburban neighborhoods, and Christian traditions. Campus activities, academic calendars, and services are designed in keeping with the holidays and celebrations of the dominant culture (Manning and Coleman-Boatwright, 1991). Even advisement techniques can reflect attitudes toward work, life-styles, or ways of coping unfamiliar to a student who is not a part of the dominant culture. While student affairs educators cannot change the campus architecture, they *can* change other aspects of college life to make it more inclusive of and familiar to multicultural students.

For students raised in nondominant cultural contexts with different sets of rules, boundaries, and modes of organization, college and community life may be incongruous (Atkinson, Morten, and Sue, 1989; McEwen, Roper,

Bryant, and Langa, 1990; Wright, 1987). For example, the formal language of academe stands in sharp contrast to the informal cultural vernacular of Black English (Kochman, 1981). Hierarchical lines of authority in higher education administration differ from those of Native American cultures where age and experience are valued (Locust, 1988).

In a study of Native Americans, Hispanics, and blacks in relation to white students, the "loss of the familiar past" (Cibik and Chambers, 1991, p. 133) on campus was felt more acutely among students of color than among whites. Native Americans, in particular, went home more often, while all students of color had difficulty forming new relationships. These students used services less, were more dissatisfied with the services that they did use, and experienced difficulty in becoming involved with formal campus organizations.

Cultural dissonance between past ways and campus ways can include college-sanctioned behaviors, manners of speaking, and styles of competition. Unlike international students who arrive at American colleges expecting cultural differences, students of color who are American may not expect their backgrounds to be acutely dissimilar from the campus culture. Rather, these students feel only a general sense of confusion, discomfort, and alienation, which undermines self-esteem and confidence and leads to social estrangement (Cook and Helms, 1991; Hayes, 1985; Jackson, 1991; Jones, Terrell, and Duggar, 1991). These feelings can be difficult to describe (Fleming, 1984), and even more challenging for student affairs educators to understand. In fact, it is the role of student affairs educators on culturally pluralistic campuses to recognize when a student is experiencing cultural dissonance and to remove barriers that thwart cultural expression.

Fleming's (1984) research on African American students in predominantly black and in predominantly white institutions provides insight into the detrimental effects of conflicts between cultural background and the norms of campus settings. This extensive study explored the confusion, helplessness, and resignation experienced by African American students at predominantly white institutions. Fleming's interpretations centered on the idea that students from cultures estranged from the dominant campus culture feel alienated and out of place.

In Fleming's study, the absence of support systems through friendships and through relationships with faculty and administrators, coupled with financial constraints and interpersonal vulnerabilities, often resulted in illness and fear of personal threat. Consequently, students were unable to gain a sense of achievement in academic pursuits. Feelings of alienation and an inability to feel part of the whole were seen by Fleming to be precipitated by this lack of support. The resulting anger and rage, not always verbally expressed, were channeled into aggressiveness and defensiveness. This pain among African American students is also evident in the literature showing a seesaw effect of enrollment and retention rates for these students (Jackson,

1991; Siggelkow, 1991). Clearly, for students of color, the goals of higher education that encompass the development of each student's potential are unfulfilled.

Take Action. Student affairs educators, among all campus participants, are faced with the responsibility of recognizing and responding to the reality that education currently requires knowledge of a wide range of cultures and ways of living and learning. The increased diversity of college campuses raises serious issues of culture and power. Many campuses no longer have homogeneous populations of students, administrators, and faculty. Students on college campuses are different not only from one another but also from the "typical" student described in the literature and research used to build management, administrative, and teaching practices (Stage, 1990). Rather than developing, learning, and reacting to administrative policies and decisions in one manner, students have *many* views of community and styles of learning. They organize their lives in a variety of ways. In general, these individual and cultural differences are not reflected in the administrative practice and formal organizational structure of colleges.

Student affairs theories are generally based on norms of monocultural populations, specifically, white upper-middle-class males (Chickering, 1969; Kohlberg, 1984; Perry, 1970). The student development theories not based on this white male population, such as articulated in Gilligan (1982) and Fleming (1984), are, again, built on research specific to a particular gender or ethnic group (women and African Americans, respectively). These theories are used to build practice, which is, again, based on monocultural norms. While this research contributes to our understanding of students, these students, as described in theory and acted upon in administrative practice, are not ethnically, sexually, racially, or culturally diverse enough to encompass the academic and personal development of all of today's students. These theories, based on generalizations, should not be *all* that we know about students (Stage, 1990). Generalizations, of use with homogeneous populations, are not appropriate with diverse, heterogeneous populations. In these latter settings, individual differences and similarities rather than group similarities should form the basis of decision making, policy-making, and administrative practice. Administration in a complex environment requires practices that respond in an individual rather than normative way.

As part of the college educational process, campus administrative practices, teaching methods, and policy-making must move toward a pluralistic approach. Do student affairs educators consciously consider various cultural perspectives when making collegewide decisions and policy? Do they administer "creatively," allowing nuances of variety in students' backgrounds to inform their policies and actions? Or do they use the same interpretation for each student under the guise of fair play? These are questions that the cultural broker must ask with the aim of developing a critical perspective on pluralistic campus cultures. This means giving up practices that assume students will conform to the norm.

The techniques needed to broaden our understanding of cultural differences and to consider the context created by the individual student are difficult, risky, and, at times, chaotic. These expanded practices entail attending to the various ways that students make sense of their environment, engaging in dialogue with students about their perspectives and their ideas, and accepting that education is a continuous process of mutual influence.

Educational and administrative practice from a culturally pluralistic perspective means decentering the dominant Eurocentric perspective and recentering the view with multiple cultures (including the Eurocentric) as the reference points. This composite perspective recognizes and celebrates the common ground among cultures (for example, social interaction, personal relationships, systems of organization). To deny any commonality of human culture and endeavors would leave educators in a hopelessly relativistic position where consensus, dialogue, and communication are impossible. Rather, the institution's culture, which reflects Eurocentric, gender-biased ideals (Katz, 1989) is broadened to include and reflect the multiplicity of styles, systems, and ways of being extant in American society. The behavioral standards, symbols, and language on campus reflect many heritages, rather than only one, of American culture.

The change in attitude, informed by cultural pluralism, in essence involves adopting a perspective that resists ethnocentrism and that goes beyond empathic listening to an understanding of the student's background, perceptual and cognitive processes, and cultural frames of reference (Weinrach, 1987). From this perspective, people of all cultures (especially the dominant) take responsibility for becoming educated about cultures different from their own. More important, they accept and celebrate other cultures with understanding and respect. A culturally informed and committed faculty and administration work to assist students in freely expressing themselves and their cultural knowledge.

Conclusion

To step outside the dominant cultural view means to trust others and to explore their perspectives and views. "Current trends are still dictated by expectations so old that they are no longer conscious" (Fleming, 1984, p. 139). Cultural brokers need to make these trends conscious, explore meaning for themselves and their students, and broaden the interpretation to include all cultures and groups.

Specific administrative procedures, policies, responses, and other management behaviors are discussed in the context of the cultural broker model.

The Administrative Role in a Diverse Environment

This chapter contains suggestions for administrative behavior that moves an organization toward multiculturalism. Several assumptions are central to the consideration of culturally sensitive administration: (1) Systemic change in organizational hierarchies and administrative structures is necessary to transform campuses into multicultural environments (Ebbers and Henry, 1990; Jaschik, 1987). (2) When culturally pluralistic interventions are an integral part of the organizational structure, care must be taken to prevent "fossilization" in the system (Bennis, 1966). (3) In this age of cultural pluralism, the long-established role of administrative authority must be reconceptualized to encompass shared power and responsibility (Freire, 1970). (4) Self-exploration of one's racial and cultural attitudes is essential for progress toward culturally sensitive practice (Ebbers and Henry, 1990; D. W. Sue and D. Sue, 1990). And (5) the dogma of multiculturalism, a threat to cultural pluralism, must be addressed by student affairs educators.

Becoming a Contextualist

The 1980s was a decade of renewed emphasis on the problem of racism. Although the need for increased numbers of underrepresented groups was widely discussed among student affairs administrators (D. Smith, 1989; Astone and Nuñez-Wormack, 1990), the reasons for supporting multiculturalism were not clearly delineated. The question, "Why multiculturalism?" requires definition and exploration. The four purposes of productivity, moral responsibility, equity, and education are offered here as bases on which student affairs administrators can establish multicultural environments.

Productivity. Students of color expend tremendous amounts of energy as they traverse predominantly white campuses (Cook and Helms, 1991). As they try to remain true to themselves, understand dominant culture ways, and negotiate campus cultural practices, they experience a burden not easily understood by dominant culture members (J. Jones, 1988). Since aspects of dominant and nondominant cultures are often at odds with one another, students of color must negotiate different cultures as well as endure the pressures of succeeding academically and socially (Cook and Helms, 1991; Fleming, 1984). The creativity and productivity possible once these burdens are removed and all students are empowered to succeed can only be imagined.

Moral Responsibility. Demographic changes have forced student affairs educators to examine campus life in the light of culturally diverse student bodies. The discussion about increases in "minority" populations frequently takes on a survival tone (Hodgkinson, 1984). Student population growth into the twenty-first century will depend on African American and Latino student recruitment (Hodgkinson, 1984; D. W. Sue, 1992). Above and beyond survival issues, multiculturalism as a philosophy and basis for administrative practice has a moral component. Multiculturalism in a morally responsible manner fulfills the equity and justice purposes of American higher education (Katz and Taylor, 1988; Sears, 1988).

Equity. The need for student affairs administrators to reconceptualize current definitions and uses of administrative authority was briefly outlined in Chapter Two. On campuses reflecting monoculturalism, authority is a vital mechanism for emphasizing one cultural perspective (for example, Eurocentric) over others (for example, Afrocentric). The goal of a reconceptualized view of administrative authority is equity.

The cultural broker's role, as proposed in this volume, borrows the idea of authority put forth by Freire (1970). He envisions the distance between the administrator and student reduced to the point where both groups are viewed as equal participants in the institution. All people are equal with respect to their humanness. This nonauthoritarian view means trusting that students can act as full participants in the campus community (Manning, 1988). A Freirean view of relationships assumes that the dualism of the administrator and the student as teacher and learner, respectively, is redefined. In that redefinition, both people are students-teachers and teachers-students in an equitable environment.

An equitable system, as described above, must consider the organizational constraints within the institution. Cultural diversity efforts on campus throughout the 1980s celebrated diversity by recognizing and giving prominence to nonmajority cultures in campus programs and services (Leppo, 1987). An equitable approach to multiculturalism means adapting existing systems and creating different, more inclusive ways of operating. This approach avoids the urge to completely demolish the existing organizational structure. Freire (1970, p. 76) calls this destruction "action for action's sake." Instead, transformation of structures is the goal. The recreation or transformation of organizations toward cultural pluralism redefines the authoritative mechanisms of the structure, challenges participants to resist silence and, instead, put words to their experience and engage in authentic dialogue.

Education. A liberal arts education employs various disciplines to answer questions and analyze situations. Multiculturalism reflects an inter-disciplinary approach by using various cultural perspectives as a lens through which to conceptualize and analyze issues. Multiculturalism as a broadened approach to liberal education incorporates perspectives previously excluded, both actively and passively, from traditional liberal arts (Giroux, 1988b; P. Smith, 1990).

The traditional American higher education curriculum is based on Western civilization with an emphasis on European culture (Aronowitz and Giroux, 1991; Botstein, 1991; W. Bennett, 1984; Bloom, 1987). In this tradition, valor, military prowess, and aggressiveness as a means to success are valued over nurturing, caring, nonviolent, and cooperative means to success (Schaef, 1985). The multidisciplinary approach of the liberal arts tradition can be reconfigured to encompass the multiple perspectives of a pluralistic society (Giroux, 1988b). In fact, in a culturally diverse society, an adequate education cannot be achieved without the inclusion of various culturally defined perspectives taught in a liberal arts tradition of interdisciplinary study.

A multicultural approach on campus urges student affairs educators to place their practice within politically, historically, and culturally defined contexts (Aronowitz and Giroux, 1991). Intimate knowledge of these contexts requires the dominant culture or white administrator to become adept at recognizing and operating within culturally defined boundaries (Ebbers and Henry, 1990; Haro, 1991; Hayes, 1985; Jones, Terrell, and Duggar, 1991).

Span Boundaries

The previous section discusses the issues related to becoming a contextualist. The second step of the cultural broker model is to span boundaries. Examples of ways that student affairs educators can span the boundaries of cultural differences in their administration are offered in the following section.

Mediation in the Face of Discipline. The treatment of black students at predominantly white institutions is frequently inconsistent, hostile, and discriminatory (Cook and Helms, 1991; Hayes, 1985). This hostile environment becomes particularly evident during roommate conflicts.

In student affairs administration, interracial roommate conflicts, a daunting problem for staff, create a lose-lose situation for students of color as well as dominant culture students. An African American student experiencing roommate conflicts based on cultural differences often must make those all too familiar feelings known to white staff who have only scant personal experience with cultural dissonance. The phrase echoed in the 1980s, "It's a cultural thing—you wouldn't understand it," reflects the gap in understanding between black and white cultures.

A change in policy to reflect more equitable approaches can rely on mediation by groups of trained staff members and students. These groups, cross-culturally composed (for example, composed of men and women from different ethnic groups), act as a source of support for students of color who are otherwise alone and underrepresented in the institutional hierarchy (Siggelkow, 1991). People composing these mediation groups can be trained to respond to situations *before* the student of color faces a sea of people who appear, at first glance, to be culturally uninformed administrators (for example, white resident director and dean's staff) or students (for example, white resident assistants). This mediation system does not replace the disciplinary process but provides a means of resolving difficulties before they escalate to the point where disciplinary intervention is necessary. The mediation system can emphasize the importance of resolving situations through the recognition of cultural differences as well as the creation of an environment where students of color feel represented in the formal administrative hierarchy. In fact, "multiracial coalitions have also been formed when campus racial tensions have boiled over, and these have generally been quite effective in uniting majority and minority students to work for common goals" (Altbach, 1991, p. 11). This approach, particularly used in advance of racial tensions, partially responds to the need for more diverse representation among faculty, students, and staff while not holding people of color solely responsible for incorporating diverse cultural perspectives into the campus environment.

Advisory Committees. Another example of boundary spanning in administrative practice is the use of advisory committees. Current practice relies on student representatives from established groups such as student governments, inter-Greek associations, and residence life organizations. Student leaders, familiar to student affairs administrators and relatively homogeneous in cultural makeup, cannot be expected to reflect the full complement of campus perspectives. Instead, student affairs educators can diligently work to incorporate cultural differences within advisory committees. The aim of these advisory committees is not to reach consensus on a particular issue but rather to communicate the diversity of campus opinions on policy issues.

Faculty, student, and administrative groups recommending changes to the campus disciplinary process, for example, need to be heterogeneously constituted in order to consider various campus perspectives. These groups, through authentic dialogue, can craft culturally sensitive responses to issues such as academic honesty, acquaintance rape, and student-on-student violence. We are not suggesting here a relativistic approach where anything is acceptable given a cultural justification. Rather, the use of heterogeneous groups reflects the realization that various student cultures have different responses to similar student issues. It is no longer realistic, if it ever was, to assume a homogeneity in responses to any one issue. Dialogue can help student affairs educators craft advisory systems that are integrated with disciplinary responses and based on well thought out approaches to the breadth of multicultural perspectives.

As many student affairs educators know, advisory committees composed of students with diverse perspectives and styles are not easily managed. The administrator must be willing to build high levels of trust among the students, give up notions of administrative control over the situation, and engage in honest dialogue with students as equals in perspective and approach to policy decisions (Gupta and Manning, 1992).

Attendance at Events. The support and advocacy activities in which student affairs staff engage when they attend events sponsored by students of color deserves mention as a significant boundary-spanning activity. Student affairs educators should actively and consistently support events of this kind every year. Direct and indirect involvement is both a symbolic representation of staff members' commitment to cultural pluralism and an excellent way to expand cultural knowledge.

Ensure Optimal Performance

In the context of this discussion, optimal performance of all students can be achieved by broadening the scope of celebrated cultural styles (Katz, 1989). After years of monocultural practice and behavior, institutions sanction and value certain cultural ways over others (Botstein, 1991). For cultural brokers seeking to span cultural boundaries, one approach is to broaden the scope of cultural styles celebrated on campus. This goal is achieved by creating opportunities for all campus participants, particularly people of color, to see themselves represented in the campus structure. Specifically, student affairs administrators must redefine the use of public space so that areas where only certain cultures, ways of operating, and manners of achievement are recognized are transformed into areas where many cultures are celebrated. Award banquets, holiday celebrations, and all-college convocations can be used in culturally inclusive rather than exclusive ways. Thus, within the structure of the institution, various cultures are equally valued and honored.

This inclusive approach to public space does not mean that administrators add multicultural events to the already overburdened calendar of campus activities. Instead, the "way things are done" is redefined to equally recognize more than one cultural perspective in everyday activities. This approach means that exclusionary practices of the majority culture are rethought (for example, Christmas decorations), significantly changed (for example, access to Greek houses), or eliminated (for example, male-only portraits hung in prominent locations) in order to achieve egalitarian use of public space.

We are not suggesting that the dominant culture is "bad" and needs to be replaced, for example, by an Afrocentric perspective. Rather, administrators are encouraged to recognize and act on current practices that exclude people from free expression of their respective cultural backgrounds within the institution.

Take Action

A multicultural approach entails a change in attitude as well as an examination of everyday actions that lead to the perpetuation of institutionalized racism (J. Jones, 1988). A multicultural approach that is *action oriented* needs to be integrated into administrative practice. This stance means that administrators representing the dominant culture must take pains to identify and understand subtle and overt forms of exclusion in their behavior as well as in programs, services, and the organizational hierarchy for which they are responsible (Fellows, 1972). This self-examination involves "an intensive study of attitudes, policies, and program practices" (Ebbers and Henry, 1990, p. 321). The focus of this volume is racism and cultural difference. Yet, the self-study must examine the effects of sexism, ageism, homophobia, and other forms of discrimination and exclusion.

The practices at issue include financial aid awards in the form of loans, when African American culture shies away from indebtedness as a means to gain education. Predominantly white staffs fail to provide substantial role-modeling opportunities for students of color (Hayes, 1985; Jones, Terrell, and Duggar, 1991). Campus dissent policies rarely take into account the historical patterns of struggle of Latinos and African Americans against established systems (Marin, 1992; Freire, 1970). Leadership programs typically emphasize individual assertiveness rather than such Latino cultural characteristics as cooperation (Arredondo, 1991) and extended family reciprocity (D. W. Sue and D. Sue, 1990). Campus calendars are based on a cycle of Christian holidays, with little or no consideration of Jewish and Moslem holidays (Manning and Coleman-Boatwright, 1991). Although student affairs administrators have taken significant strides toward multicultural celebration, the continuation of some practices inadvertently excludes diverse students from everyday campus life. Overall, an action-oriented approach to multiculturalism should consider issues such as cross-cultural communication, conflict management and privilege, dissent policies, and personnel issues.

Communication and Inclusive Language. As discussed in Chapter Two, dialogue is the centerpiece of any cross-cultural communication effort. Dialogue, as opposed to agreement or consensus building, is aimed toward understanding the "other" (Freire, 1970). When cross-cultural understanding is present, actions to create equitable systems are possible.

The task of building relationships between predominantly white administrators and people of color means adopting language that is more inclusive than generally used in everyday conversation. These efforts are difficult given the prevalence of jargon and "academese" prevalent on campuses. Since language use reflects one's philosophy of social interaction, it is essential that student affairs administrators use words that include rather than exclude, so that the multicultural perspective of the administrator is recognized by those listening.

The discussion here is not intended to support a politically correct perspective (Adler and others, 1990; Mackenzie, 1991; Steele, 1990; Taylor, 1991). *Politically correct* is a "pejorative term for a pattern of behavior in which discourse, argument, and good sense are stifled by an imposed conformity that places maximum value on giving no offense to such 'marginalized' groups as women, people of color, gays and lesbians, Jews, Muslims, and the poor" (Mackenzie, 1991, p. B1). Rather, dialogue is based on critical considerations of the advantages and disadvantages of various cultural perspectives (Katz, 1989; Manning and Coleman-Boatwright, 1991).

Communication issues are complex because speech patterns are so ingrained in one's style of social interaction that change is difficult and, at times, painful. The achievement of a multicultural environment means that student affairs administrators recognize the ways that language oppresses as well as closes down dialogue among people divided by cultural differences.

Conflict Management and Privilege. Another immediate action toward multiculturalism is conflict management. The methods associated with cultural diversity (for example, recruitment of faculty and staff of color) result in a shift in the power configuration and distribution of privileges on campuses (J. Jones, 1988). Prior to the civil rights movement and cultural diversity initiatives, privileges were inequitably distributed in favor of the white majority. For example, whites have greater access to higher education through mentoring and encouragement during the lower educational levels. Jobs are more available to whites because the absence of discrimination against their race bestows unproven attributions of competence. Academic achievement is more likely because of less threat of violence against them. Few white students fight against the stigma of being labeled an "affirmative action" college entrant.

The notion of privilege among dominant culture members (J. Jones, 1988) is complex and not easily recognized by college students. The current system of white privilege has been intact for so long that those who benefit from it assume that privileges are rights. When privileges are defined as rights, it is difficult, at times impossible, to recognize the inequities inherent to the system. Any change from the distribution of privilege currently favoring whites is not always perceived as a move toward equity for people of color *and* whites. Rather, the changes are typically construed by whites as a denial of privileges to which they have become accustomed. Any change that moves students of color toward equity is often perceived as "reverse discrimination" by dominant culture students. These misunderstandings fuel the backlash against multicultural interventions. The shift in privilege and the resulting backlash are clearly evident in the myths surrounding affirmative action hiring and admissions.

The situation of privilege is even more complex when viewed from the perspective of students of color (Steele, 1990). "Special programs for black students tend to frustrate them and have a negative effect on their achievement, because many blacks feel they are being isolated and singled out because they are 'not as good as' the white students" (Hayes, 1985, p. 48).

Dissent Policies. Historically the design of higher education is to discover new knowledge and, in principle at least, progress toward social equity (P. Smith, 1990). Accompanying these goals has been institutional members' responsibility to question and assess their efforts for social equity. Dissent is part and parcel of a campus life that questions dogmatic teachings as well as celebrates an environment where new ideas are conceived, discussed, and established (Horowitz, 1986).

The importance of instituting policies and procedures of inclusion *prior to* culturally motivated action by any campus group cannot be overestimated. These "efforts must be continuing and sustained, rather than periodic and crisis oriented" (Siggelkow, 1991, p. 102). The intentions of administrators are justifiably suspect if policies are instituted or adapted in the midst of a campus crisis. When policies are written and adopted in advance, they can serve as a basis of dialogue on the goals of multiculturalism, resolve differences in opinion about the appropriate means toward these ends, and involve community members on all sides of the issue in discussion about potential protests and other acts of dissent. A priori policy formation creates educational opportunities for students, board of trustee members, faculty, and administrators.

Of course, policies formulated with the best of intentions cannot discourage the efforts of students who are determined to make a statement or disrupt the campus. Three hundred years of practice with student dissent (Horowitz, 1986) has not resulted in easy answers about its resolution (Miser, 1988). The management of these difficult campus events as educational opportunities for all students remains a daunting challenge.

Staff Issues. A substantial portion of the student affairs literature discusses the importance of recruiting and hiring people of color as faculty and administrators (Ebbers and Henry, 1990; Hayes, 1985; Jaschik, 1987; Jones, Terrell, and Duggar, 1991; Strong, 1988). Because these resources are readily available, the practice of hiring people of color as an aspect of multiculturalism is not discussed in this volume. Instead, we examine structural and systemic issues of supervision and training.

Supervision. A "multicultural management style is . . . the purposeful recognition and affirmation of unique personal cultural attributes brought into the workplace by each employee" (Strong, 1988, p. 1). This approach differs markedly from the commonly misunderstood practice of affirmative action. Affirmative action is routinely used to perpetuate the myth that people of color require special circumstances to succeed (Steele, 1990). The assumption under such an arrangement is that people of color do not have the skills or attributes needed to benefit the organization. Therefore, they would not be hired without affirmative action measures. This misinterpretation of affirmative action perpetuates the myth that people of color have less to offer an organization than do dominant culture persons. In lieu of this myth, employers and supervisors must recognize characteristics and attributes that are different from those of the white, predominantly male majority norm but are of equal value to the organization (Astin, 1989; Hayes, 1985; Strong, 1988).

A multicultural approach to supervision assumes that *all* people have attributes that are of value and can benefit the institution (Katz, 1989; Manning and Coleman-Boatwright, 1991). Furthermore, it is the responsibility of the student affairs supervisor to continue efforts to take down barriers that limit the expression of these talents (Astin, 1989). Student affairs educators are often well practiced at creating opportunities for culturally diverse attributes to be utilized and valued within the organization. The goal of increased cultural competence of all staff (Ebbers and Henry, 1990) is a primary objective of student affairs staffs across the country. This goal incorporates the belief that a diversity of skills and attributes in the organization leads to better decision making, policymaking, and increased creativity and productivity (Katz, 1989). Culturally sensitive supervisors are knowledgeable about the culturally unique skills and attributes of different groups, build meaningful dialogues about how these unique skills and attributes can be expressed, and celebrate diverse management styles within the departments for which they are responsible (Strong, 1988).

Training. Given the limited sustained intercultural interaction in American society (Jones, Terrell, and Duggar, 1991), culturally sensitive administration is rarely achieved without specialized training. The current predominance of monocultural perspectives (Schaef, 1985) is pervasive and difficult to recognize without assistance.

Student affairs administrators can no longer assume that willingness to understand multiculturalism means understanding or that theoretical understanding without contact is enough (Claney and Parker, 1989; J. Jones, 1988). Instead, there must be a system of realistic assessment of administrators' skills. For example, an assumption of multicultural understanding coupled with a willingness to teach seminars, workshops, and race and culture classes cannot be substituted for expertise in those areas. Multicultural issues must be treated as any other area of expertise in terms of the need for assessment and training before competence can be correctly assumed. In fact, similar to counseling, stringent standards for expertise should be exercised in this area since misunderstanding is commonplace and the opportunities for irreparable damage are frequent. The student affairs field should consider the practices of cross-cultural counseling, where it is unethical to engage in therapy with a person who is ethnically or culturally different from oneself without first understanding the implications of those cultural differences (Atkinson, Morten, and Sue, 1989; D. W. Sue, 1992; D. W. Sue and D. Sue, 1990). "To understand the world view of the minority client, counselors must learn about the client's culture and about how the sociopolitical system in the United States operates with respect to its treatment of minorities. Along with this understanding, counselors must have a clear and explicit knowledge of the characteristics of counseling that may be both culture-bound and class-bound. The greater the depth of knowledge of our culturally diverse groups and the more knowledge we have of many groups, the more likely we are to be effective helpers" (D. W. Sue, 1992, p. 13).

Remove Barriers. The final immediate action recommended as student affairs administrators take action toward multiculturalism is to remove the barriers that thwart multiculturalism within the institutional structure (Colon, 1991; Sears, 1988). "Colleges must make radical changes in their structure, values, hiring practices, and the way they treat students if they want to attract more minority students and professors to their institutions" (Jaschik, 1987, p. 1). The task of removing these barriers to achievement for people of color means that administrators must "reexamine themselves constantly" (Freire, 1970, p. 47) in light of the realization that racism is a fundamental part of institutional life (Barr and Strong, 1988; Fellows, 1972; J. Jones, 1988; Katz and Taylor, 1988; Sears, 1988).

Student affairs administrators who have significant responsibility for large portions of administration, particularly of student life, often recognize but have not fully embraced their role in the creation of egalitarian systems. Meaningful change toward the goal of multiculturalism can result from the creation of pockets of multiculturalism in student affairs areas. This grass-roots action can be undertaken at both individual and organizational levels and have significant impact. Many of the programming and educational efforts of the 1980s initiated this effort. The current momentum of student affairs educators promises to evolve into continued institutional efforts. The mechanisms through which institutionalized racism is perpetuated can be turned around to recreate egalitarian, multicultural systems.

Summary

Student affairs administrators who are struggling as cultural brokers can ponder the following questions: What actions can administrators take even when a commitment does not exist within other areas of the institution? How does the push to reach consensus about the outcomes and goals of multiculturalism delay meaningful actions to achieve cultural pluralism? How does well-established and tutored cultural distrust impede cross-cultural relationships defined by honest communication and dialogue? Has the "politically correct" movement goaded student affairs administrators to attest or disavow their commitment to multiculturalism? What mechanisms cause administrators to, at worst, deny and, at best, reluctantly admit their ignorance about issues of cultural difference? Have we fallen into the trap of easy stereotyping, however noble our intentions, in the name of "cultural awareness"? The process of becoming a cultural broker means discovering territory previously not seen. This "terrain is uneven, full of sudden faults and dangerous passages where accidents can and do happen, and crossing it, or trying to, does little or nothing to smooth it out to a level, safe, unbroken plain, but simply makes visible its clefts and contours" (Geertz, 1986, p. 119). Recognizing the contours of the terrain is often more painful and dangerous than tripping on them unseen. But the historical charge to the student affairs field concerning the growth of *all* students precludes any refusal to take this journey.

Frequently, problems of diversity arise in the college classroom. This chapter discusses acceptance of various learning styles, abilities, and cultures in relationship to flexibility in working with students in the classroom.

Academic Concerns in a Diverse Environment

Colleges and universities are well known for their imperviousness to change. In fact, that reluctance to change is frequently cited as a reason for their survival among the world's oldest institutions. In the United States, campus traditions have been carried on for over 350 years, following the traditions, styles, and expectations that first were developed in Britain and Germany in the fifteenth and sixteen centuries. Architectural styles persist as well. New campuses continue to be built around quadrangles of green with appurtenant clock towers and ivy. Huge campuses are planned and administered as megacommunities long after sociology and psychology have told us that students fare better in smaller settings (Barker, 1968).

In addition to the edifices and expectations described above, Eurocentric roots run deeper. Timeworn notions of the faculty as an elite community of scholars and of the student as a receptor of knowledge are embodied in the classroom. In lectures and in the imitation style of learning that is expected in mathematics and the sciences, the assumption is that the "scholar" holds the knowledge to be imparted to the student. Classroom styles and expectations have firm bases in Eurocentric ways of thinking, processing information, and learning (Anderson, 1988; Katz, 1989; Manning, 1992; Stage, 1992a). Classroom communication most often reflects traditions of standard English and writing, direct eye contact, and controlled emotions.

These traditions and expectations are unsurprising to many students who arrive at college campuses, eager to begin their college careers. However, they might come as a surprise to a student from a predominantly African American community whose high school teacher encouraged emotional reactions to literature and journalism and who encouraged students to respond in a colloquial fashion in the classroom (Katz, 1989). Likewise, the emphasis of the world history class on European-American history might be disappointing to the Asian-American student. The continued persistence of these expectations and styles is disadvantageous to those who do as well as do not share the Eurocentric culture.

In this chapter, we discuss strategies for incorporating the cultural backgrounds and styles of all students into academic planning and expectations. One way this can be done is by expanding sources of class materials and topics to include more diverse perspectives. A second way is by considering variations in college students' styles of processing information. Finally, we discuss ways for student affairs staff to overcome obstacles to the establishment of a multicultural academic environment.

Classroom Materials

In addition to the edifices, rituals, and ways of behaving of the academy described above, Eurocentric bias is manifest in classroom materials in three ways: overt prejudice, unrealistic perspectives, and lack of inclusiveness.

Overt prejudice was once common on college campuses. It can include stereotyping and derogatory language. It might include assigning traditional or rigid roles or attributes to a particular group. It might also include the use of derogatory terminology and racially loaded words and phrases to present issues.

Unrealistic perspectives can include selectivity and imbalance in course materials. Issues may be presented and interpreted from only one perspective, or there may be an unrealistic portrayal of history through avoidance of touchy subjects.

Lack of inclusiveness may be the most insidious form of bias because it is usually not obvious, especially to unsophisticated scholars. It can occur when certain groups are not represented or barely represented in materials. Lack of inclusiveness also can occur when multicultural issues are addressed as an "add on" to regular class materials, whereby the issues appear to be afterthoughts or unworthy of incorporation into the main materials of the class.

Unfortunately, it is not difficult to think of instances on campus when such biases occur. For example, in traditional history, psychology, and literature courses, multicultural experiences and perspectives are frequently excluded. Historical events such as black slavery, World War II internment of Japanese Americans, and Native American relocations are presented and interpreted from only one perspective. The lack of civil rights for gays and lesbians and federal budget cuts that systematically disfavor single mothers are nonissues. Often they are not considered serious topics for scholarship, the classroom, or a student's research paper.

Traditional ways of choosing and presenting materials as well as of evaluating learning reflect a lifetime of conditioning for those who employ them. For many raised in the American Eurocentric culture, traditional learning styles were taught before they entered school as well as reinforced throughout their education (Heath, 1983; Manning, 1987). Since these individuals populate the college and university faculties, it is not surprising that assumptions about what is important to learn, how learning should take place, and how students should convey information derive from the Eurocentric perspective. Operationalization of those assumptions, through a textbook chosen, a topic covered, and a syllabus constructed, does not necessarily produce the absolute criteria for learning. Rather, the product is just one of many ways of learning. There are other, equally effective ways.

As discussed in previous chapters, the campus no longer is populated only by those who share the American Eurocentric culture. This change in the college student population provides an opportunity for students, faculty, and administrators to become more flexible and creative in ways of thinking about learning inside and outside the classroom. It is time to expand repertoires of communication and learning and to explore the wealth of materials and knowledge of those whose cultures differ from the Eurocentric worldview. In short, it is time to add exciting new elements to tired curricula.

Faculty, who are among the most stressed individuals in the college environment, often seem too busy, too set in their established patterns of doing things, to create the kind of depth and flexibility in the learning setting that provide an optimal learning experience for all students. Often, it is student affairs educators who must raise the consciousness of others on the college campus.

Information-Processing Issues

Shade (1982) reviewed the literature of cultural diversity and psychological, cognitive, and behavioral strategies in school. African American students typically differed from comparison groups in terms of cognitive style and were at a disadvantage in classrooms where other styles were valued, encouraged, and used as the bases for communicating and learning. For example, some studies found that African American students, when compared with students of other ethnic subgroups, performed better on verbal memory tasks, but worse on space conceptualization tasks (Leifer, 1972; Lesser, Fifer, and Clark, 1965; Stodolsky and Lesser, 1967). Researchers in other studies also found cognitive style differences between middle and lower socioeconomic status African Americans. For the variable of field independence, which relates to an individual's ability to look at a set of information and scan and focus on particular elements, African Americans of lower socioeconomic status demonstrated greater field dependence (Orasanu, Lee, and Scribner, 1979; Sigel, Anderson, and Shapiro, 1966).

Kolb (1985) developed a typology describing learning styles of students in four categories: convergers, divergers, assimilators, and accommodators.

Convergers are most comfortable with abstract concepts and active experimentation. They prefer practical applications of ideas, rarely exhibit emotion, and usually have specific interests. Divergers are most comfortable with concrete experience and reflective observation, often have vivid imaginations, and are able to view concrete situations from a variety of perspectives. Assimilators learn most effectively through abstract conceptualization and reflective observation. They excel in work with theoretical models and inductive reasoning. Accommodators learn best in settings that allow for concrete experience and active experimentation; they prefer doing to thinking. Accommodators rely heavily on information from other people rather than theories, are very adaptable, and solve problems intuitively.

Kolb's work and other related research has important implications for the creation of a multicultural campus environment. Researchers have documented learning style differences in the college classroom (Russell and Rothschadl, 1991). It is unsurprising that most faculty members tend to be assimilators. Abstract conceptualization and reflective observation, characteristic of assimilators, are assets for those who must "publish or perish." Those styles of thinking and learning heavily influence classroom assignments and evaluations on a typical college campus. Students who match the instructor's style are apt to feel most comfortable, and to be most successful, in the college classroom. Those who do not match may not have opportunities to use their own dominant learning styles to their advantage. Rothschadl and Russell (1992) provide suggestions for faculty who seek to broaden the range of student learning styles that can be accommodated in their classrooms.

Anderson (1988) discussed the ways that differences in various ethnically diverse students' and majority students' learning styles might affect success in college. He also discussed the learning strengths of many students from particular ethnic groups. Many majority students are comfortable with the abstract theory and reflective observation (assimilators) that typify college classroom learning. However, many multicultural students learn more easily with concrete examples and practical application, characteristic of divergers. Class and culture are apparently part of the explanation for these learning style differences (Heath, 1983). Anderson concluded that a variety of teaching and evaluation techniques are needed to facilitate learning for all students.

Other research has specified the ways in which Native American and Latino students differ from majority students in their cognitive approaches to mathematical learning tasks (Charbonneau and John-Steiner, 1988; Cocking and Mestre, 1988; Leap, 1988). In most cases, classroom material was presented to students in ways that did not capitalize on the students' own unique ways of learning. Frequently, when presentational style was changed to match the multicultural students' styles, learning was enhanced.

The Student Affairs Professional as Cultural Broker

When student affairs administrators are acting as educators and promoting cultural pluralism, it is most often in their work with individual students or with student groups in the cocurriculum (Brown, 1989); often, the academic side of the campus is forgotten. However, it is frequently the student affairs administrator who must serve as broker between a faculty member who is rooted firmly in tradition and the diverse students that he or she serves. Zeller, Hinni, and Eison (1989) wrote about the increasing importance of the partnership between academics and student affairs.

For example, in the first vignette of Chapter One, we read about Carmen, an international student who had been recruited to her college as a member of an athletic team. Carmen was having academic difficulties because of her level of English proficiency, something that Professor Brown did not consider. The professor apparently made several assumptions that served to disadvantage Carmen. He assumed that her absences were unexcused, that her language ability was sufficient to communicate effectively in an essay exam, and that his provision of alternative ways of demonstrating learning could be construed as providing an unfair advantage to particular students.

An academic adviser, apprised of the situation, might serve as an advocate for Carmen. But the administrator, counselor, or adviser who is helping to create a multicultural campus faces the additional responsibility in this situation of considering not only his or her own and the student's perspectives but the perspective of the professor involved. This kind of brokerage may be delicate because it entails working with faculty within their domain, without encroaching on the turf of the classroom. Faculty are understandably protective of their hard-earned academic freedom. Attempts at intervention must take this factor into account. Student affairs educators must be aware of their limitations; their job is not to tell faculty how to teach. But as cultural brokers they can provide faculty with invaluable information about multicultural college students that may help to resolve situations inside and outside the classroom where cultural pluralism is at issue.

In today's complex campus environment, many difficult academic issues are confronted by those who are brokers between the academic realm and diverse students. A frequent debate on many campuses centers on quality of students admitted versus unlimited access. Highly competitive schools hold fast to traditional ways of evaluating prospective students, thereby ensuring relatively homogeneous student bodies. Other campuses elect to bring to campus diverse students who do not "match" in terms of preparation, orientation, or modes of participation. When campuses are not modified effectively to serve these students, cycles of attrition and achievement-diversity concerns occur (Richardson and Skinner, 1990). While student affairs professionals may not have much voice in how this recruitment issue is resolved, student affairs educators as cultural brokers can provide administrators and faculty with a more complete picture of such issues.

For example, advocates for quality often presume that quantitative test scores are closely linked with the scholastic ability of students. Studies have demonstrated that for women, and even more so for ethnic minority students, quantitative test scores do not clearly correlate with performance in college (Powell and Steelman, 1984; Stage, 1992a). Those who hold fast to traditional admissions criteria for prospective students may not be fairly evaluating the potential of diverse students.

Finally, increasingly on today's college campuses, faculty and staff are working with students who have been diagnosed as learning disabled (Mangrum and Strichart, 1984; Milne, 1989). Most faculty, who typically have no formal education on teaching methods and techniques, know very little about college students with learning disabilities. These students, who are counseled to talk with their professors about their special needs, sometimes present the undereducated faculty member with a dilemma. The student affairs administrator can sometimes fill this "educational gap." There are other classroom-related issues as well.

The student affairs professional can serve as cultural broker on campus by informing faculty of differences in learning styles and abilities. Circulation of copies of articles or research briefs that include summaries and source citations as well as suggestions for alternative teaching and evaluation strategies can raise faculty members' consciousness of their own assumptions about student learning styles.

One of the authors of this volume was once on the mathematics faculty of a community college. The student affairs staff regularly distributed one- or two-page missives to all faculty on a variety of topics, many of which were new to this mathematics instructor: research on acceptable social distance for students of various cultures, special facilities and procedures for helping students with disabilities, tips for teaching students with hearing impairments, and research examining the effect of varying response times on number of student responses to questions in the classroom. One immediate result was an improvement in the mathematics instructor's style and awareness of individuals in her classroom. A long-term result was a doctorate with a focus on college students rather than on mathematics.

Many large college campuses have a faculty development unit; this office provides faculty with information on how to improve their teaching, research, and time management skills, and information on other aspects of their diverse responsibilities. By developing a collegial relationship with staff in the faculty development unit, student affairs educators may be able to establish another area of influence. Often, faculty development offices welcome workshops for faculty that address learning styles, student development issues, and variables relating to increased flexibility in the classroom.

The Cultural Broker Model for Faculty

The cultural broker model can serve as a means for educating faculty about the assumptions that they make when working with college students. A workshop or a brief handout can introduce faculty to the four steps of the model: learning to think contextually, boundary spanning, ensuring optimal performance, and taking action. As part of an introduction to the model, faculty could be asked to examine the assumptions that are made about learning in a typical college classroom and how these assumptions can disenfranchise a growing number of their students. Faculty also could talk about their own modes of presentation and ways of evaluating students. Kolb (1985) or another learning style theory could be used as a basis for pointing out the consistency with which the participants' classroom emphasis is on one or two major styles. A discussion could ensue on the disadvantages for students with alternative styles.

The next part of the workshop or a brochure could focus on alternative ways of learning. This segment would also point out research demonstrating consistent stylistic differences across cultural groupings (Anderson, 1988; Katz, 1989; Shade, 1982). Exercises on ways of modifying modes of presentation could also be conducted (Knefelkamp, 1974; Rothschadl and Russell, 1992).

The third step is the most creative aspect of the process: brainstorming about ways to be more inclusive in materials chosen, style of presentation, and evaluation of learning in college classes. For example, presentation of materials in a variety of formats and use of a variety of modes in student assignments (oral presentations, written papers, and test performance) may be common elements in excellent teachers' classrooms. In these classrooms, multicultural students' diverse presentational styles and unique cultural information are viewed as assets (Blake, 1985) that help faculty members and their students share in the learning experience.

Individuals who have been honored for their teaching excellence can serve as catalysts in the generation of ideas for new ways of doing things in the classroom. At this point in the workshop, it is important to remind faculty that they cannot make traditional assumptions about the educational needs of ethnically diverse students in their classes (Higbee, 1991). By broadening the accepted presentational and work styles of a classroom, we are making learning better for all students.

Finally, faculty who have developed flexible classrooms with multiple modes of learning can also serve as cultural brokers within their own departments and schools. They have learned to be aware of the assumptions that they make about knowledge and learning as well as to broaden their notions of acceptable scholarship. Ideally, their own examples and influence will gradually create inroads of change toward multiculturalism in the academy.

It is easy to think of scenarios in the academic arena where a multicultural student is disadvantaged. A professor grading class exams notices that two Middle Eastern students, who always seem to be together in class, have written nearly identical answers on an essay question. He was in the classroom during the exam but was working on a paper and did not really pay close attention to the class. He assumed that his presence would thwart any collaboration. He is unsure of what to do in this situation. In his discomfort, he ends up grading their responses much more strictly than he would have had their answers been different from one another.

It might seem natural for this professor, who probably has assumptions about the competitive nature and individual effort style of most American students, to question the veracity of the students' answers. What he may not know is that it is not unusual for many international students to share notes and study together. It is not unlikely that the students might bring nearly identical information into an exam. Had the professor been aware of alternative learning styles, he probably would have questioned them about the way in which they studied for the exam before grading their papers.

Conclusion

Professor Brown in the first vignette of Chapter One was faced with a dilemma regarding Carmen, a Spanish-speaking athlete, who was having academic difficulty in one of her classes. The professor was probably overburdened with the responsibilities of a large lecture class. Nevertheless, he did not take the time to learn about Carmen's circumstances, which would have provided legitimate reasons for the missed classes. Perhaps Carmen, as an international student, shy about approaching the instructor, used the request for extra credit as a general plea for help in the class. The professor also ignored signs of language difficulty and did not consider alternative ways of testing Carmen.

In an alternate scenario, an advocate for Carmen could have suggested reasonable response alternatives to Professor Brown. While extra credit might not be a reasonable alternative, perhaps Carmen could take an incomplete in the course and sit in again the following semester, when she would not be traveling with her team. Or perhaps Professor Brown, with more information on Carmen's linguistic proficiency limitations, could reexamine her previously graded papers. Perhaps her language difficulties did not constitute serious course deficiencies but, amidst 150 class papers, were hastily graded low. As a final alternative, perhaps Carmen could take a makeup exam or her final exam in her native language, Spanish. These are the kinds of alternatives that an unsophisticated student might not think of but that an experienced professional broker between the faculty member and the student easily develops.

In an ideal scenario, with Professor Brown as a cultural broker, perhaps such issues would not have arisen. Professor Brown presents material in a multitude of ways for his class. He avails himself of a broad array of classroom media and requires outside reading assignments of his own and students' choosing. Additionally, students demonstrate their learning in a variety of ways. In their small groups they make one presentation, have other opportunities to speak aloud, and do numerous in-class reaction papers. They write several short papers and have essay as well as objective questions on their tests. In this classroom, all students have the opportunity to use a variety of skills and talents to express their learning.

Summary

Frequently, there are hindrances to the application of the cultural broker model. Some faculty might believe they are too busy to spend time on anything except what is immediately relevant to their disciplines. Others might not be receptive to suggestions for change in their classroom behavior. Still others might believe that students who cannot grasp material in the manner in which it is presented are not intelligent enough to be in college. Fortunately, faculty holding opinions such as these seem to be decreasing in number. Many faculty are receptive to suggestions for change, interested in information on student learning, and willing to adjust their habits and styles once they understand the issues involved.

Finally, there are many avenues for change that the student affairs administrator as cultural broker can pursue. Frequently, planning committees for academic areas of institutions require staff members as members of those groups. The tasks of serving on curriculum committees, teaching freshman seminar courses, and participating in planning efforts are all constructive ways for the cultural broker to positively affect the academic environment.

This chapter discusses how student affairs educators can work with students to achieve multicultural goals. A particularly untapped resource on campus, majority student leaders, is placed in the context of the institution's movement toward multiculturalism.

Multicultural Implications for Students

Several assumptions about student affairs educators and student groups underlie the administrative practices suggested in this chapter: (1) Administrators must avoid both relativism (for example, culture is valued for culture's sake) and stereotyping in their work with students (Manning and Coleman-Boatwright, 1991). (2) College campuses are hostile environments for people of color (Colon, 1991; Cook and Helms, 1991; Fleming, 1984; Hayes, 1985; Helms, 1991; Siggelkow, 1991). (3) Student affairs educators play a pivotal role in campus efforts to achieve multiculturalism (Ebbers and Henry, 1990). (4) Dominant culture students differ vastly from students of color in their knowledge of and commitment to multiculturalism (Claney and Parker, 1989). (5) Problems encountered by students of color have political and societal origins rather than only individual personal sources (Atkinson, Morten, and Sue, 1989; Colon, 1991; D. W. Sue and D. Sue, 1990). (6) Culture is not deterministic but acts as one of many influences on the student.

Learn to Think Contextually

The cultural broker model, as in previous chapters, will be used to examine roles and purposes that students can serve on campus. Learn to think contextually is the first step of that model.

Recognizing a Hostile Environment. In light of recurring racial incidents on campus, student affairs educators are safe in assuming that the campus is hostile for students of color (Colon, 1991; Fleming, 1984; Hayes, 1985; Siggelkow, 1991; D. W. Sue and D. Sue, 1990). African Americans, in particular, have been the targets of hate on campus. "Black Americans are no longer fighting for the right to attend White universities, but Black students are finding that often White campuses are hostile environments that harbor sentiments of 'old' racism" (Cook and Helms, 1991, p. 74). But Asian

Americans have also been the targets of racially motivated hate crimes (Chan and Wang, 1991; D. W. Sue and D. Sue, 1990). The low graduation rates of Latinos point to areas of concern about the campus environment for this cultural group as well (Astone and Nuñez-Wormack, 1990; Chan and Wang, 1991; Hayes, 1985; Solomon and Wingard, 1991).

In response to the effects of this hostile environment, many administrators have sought to increase the number (in other words, cultural diversity) of people of color in faculty and administrative positions on campus. With these efforts, they hope to provide mentors and role models for students of color (Siggelkow, 1991). In addition, an increased number of people of color in positions of power may shift the balance of power in the campus environment (Aronowitz and Giroux, 1991; Giroux, 1988b).

Increases in the numbers of administrators from underrepresented groups are part but not all of the solution to the problem of hostile campus environments. All faculty, students, and staff, regardless of race, gender, or ethnicity, and regardless of whether through role modeling of multicultural behavior or through cross-cultural mentoring, must help create a more multicultural, inclusive environment. Dominant culture administrators willing to take the risks to build a multicultural institution can be hired, trained, and entrusted to work toward multiculturalism. This solution recognizes that racism is a problem for all cultures and ethnic groups (Katz, 1989).

Since, in a hostile environment, students of color confront ethnic and cultural issues that can be shared *only* within the safety and comfort of ethnically related groups, culturally defined support groups (for example, Black Greeks) play an extremely important role in campus life (Cook and Helms, 1991; Altbach, 1991). Despite their success in helping to retain students of color on campus, these groups have been soundly criticized as promoting a "politically correct" environment on campus. They are said to fragment the campus, promote segregation, and work to disadvantage students of color (Steele, 1990). But, critics of these so-called Balkanized groups fail to understand that students need their support in order to defend themselves against the hostile campus environment. The academic and personal success of many students may depend on their ability to discover groups in which they can safely share their fears, successes, and ways of being.

Critics of these groups also fail to acknowledge that ethnically defined groups have a long history of campus and community involvement. Through cultural celebrations, speakers, and advocacy, black student unions, Latino organizations, and other efforts, ethnic groups have worked independently as well as with student affairs professionals to significantly increase educational efforts to achieve multiculturalism. The students leading these groups fulfill a role that majority students are not required to undertake: educating the campus community about their respective cultures. Majority students see their culture represented in countless ways across the institution.

Students of color have, in concert with student affairs staff and alone, educated, cajoled, struggled, and demanded multicultural representation in the institution.

The cultural broker's role with these support groups is to understand their functions and to remove barriers (for example, bureaucratic red tape on funding, space and policy restrictions) to their success. With an understanding of the support groups, the cultural broker can defend, when necessary, and communicate, when possible, their purposes to students, faculty, and other administrators. This communication includes debunking of myths about isolationism and correcting misunderstandings about the purposes of ethnically defined groups. Communication is essential in the face of white backlash (for example, formation of white student unions), whereby these groups are viewed as special privileges rather than as survival mechanisms.

Culturally Sensitive Leadership Styles. The student affairs educator who acts as a cultural broker needs a variety of administrative styles in order to work effectively with diverse cultural groups. African American students may have a more vocal, passionate communication style (Kochman, 1981; Phelps, Meara, Davis, and Patton, 1991). Asian American students may be reluctant to speak freely on the presence of an adviser who is an "elder" and therefore highly respected in their cultures (Astone and Nuñez-Wormack, 1990; Chung and Okazaki, 1991; D. W. Sue and D. Sue, 1990, 1991; Tomine, 1991). Native American students may avoid eye contact in the presence of an administrator (Locust, 1988). Using a multicultural approach in an ethnically diverse environment, administrators as cultural brokers understand how historical circumstances of culture influence leadership styles. They not only become adept at recognizing and valuing diverse leadership styles but also learn and incorporate diverse styles into their own repertoires, styles that may not fit the majority culture view of leadership. Other cultural styles, which also may not fit the majority culture worldview, are also learned and incorporated into the cultural broker's repertoire. Who are the heroes and heroines in other cultures? How does culture influence a student's communication style? What are the areas of conflict and congruence across cultures that can lead to misunderstanding and understanding?

Kochman (1981) provides examples of how particular cultures take different, sometimes opposite, approaches to communication. He contends that the African American passionate and persuasive style contrasts sharply with the white culture preference for objective, rational speech and argument. In his analysis, it is no surprise that people who are strongly influenced by African American culture and those strongly influenced by white culture have trouble understanding one another.

Analyses such as Kochman's should not be used to stereotype the behaviors of students of color. Respect for the student's individual approach to cultural issues warrants an understanding of the person in relation to his or her culture, not the culture in relation to the person. To see only the culture and not the student is as insensitive to that person's needs as ignoring the culture completely.

Heritage Consistency and Inconsistency. Each student of color is unique in the way that he or she embraces aspects of culture. Recognizing this uniqueness, the cultural broker does not assume that a student raised in a particular culture blindly adheres to the cultural values and ways of that culture. Even if a student is highly heritage consistent (Atkinson, Morten, and Sue, 1989), one cannot assume that he or she adheres to *all* cultural practices. It is insulting and demeaning for administrators to only view a student of color as a product of his or her culture rather than as a product of the choices that he or she makes about that culture. Individual differences as well as group cultural issues must be taken into account through authentic dialogue. This critical perspective is maintained by the cultural broker in dialogue with the student about issues of culture. What has the student adopted from his or her cultural background? What does the student know about his or her cultural background? What are the student's feelings about cultural issues?

Assessment of the heritage consistency of a student is extremely difficult. Influences of the dominant culture are so strong that students of color, women, and other nonmajority students may not know what pieces of cultural history are missing from their repertoires of knowledge (Cook and Helms, 1991; Freire, 1970). If they are heritage consistent, confusion still ensues because dominant culture messages about what to believe or not believe create difficulties as the student decides which cultural traditions to embrace and which to reject. The cultural broker must assume that students of color are not static in their feelings, their opinions, and their adherence to cultural ways.

College is a significant period of cultural and racial discovery for traditionally aged students (Claney and Parker, 1989). Due to the circumstance of limited sustained social interaction among racial groups (Fellows, 1972; J. Jones, 1988; Jones, Terrell, and Duggar, 1991; Sears, 1988), college may be the first setting in which students, white as well as students of color, interact and work closely with people different from themselves. Differences in educational background and experience may be more explicit than previously encountered in predominantly white or predominantly black neighborhoods.

With the expansion of theoretical choices within curricula (for example, feminist theory, ethnic studies, non-Western approaches, new paradigm research), students may be overwhelmed in their discovery of perspectives never considered before college. These new perspectives, in addition to messages about diversity communicated and debated on campus, may raise issues not previously explored by dominant culture students and students of color. College may be the first time that issues of race, ethnicity, and gender are explored.

The diverse opinions and perspectives that exist on campus make clear that the majority view once accepted as preeminent is no longer the only perspective available (Aronowitz and Giroux, 1991; Giroux, 1988b). These contested and often conflicting points of view have created a situation that many educators view as problematic and in need of resolution in favor of a Western perspective (W. Bennett, 1984; Bloom, 1987; Hirsch, 1987). The higher education literature is full of laments for a return to a simpler age when only one point of view was favored. The cultural broker must not only resist these pleas for simplicity but also support the multiplicity of perspectives presently put forth on campus. The monoculturalism of the system (that is, predominance of the Western perspective) is now being openly discussed and debated.

Span Boundaries

The boundary spanning of the cultural broker role is perhaps the most important consideration as student affairs educators work with students. Interracial boundaries between African American and white roommates are crossed in conflict negotiation. Communication boundaries are crossed when a lower-level administrator interprets students' needs for the upper echelon of administration. Staff-to-staff boundaries are crossed as people with cultural knowledge share that resource with others. Teacher-learner boundaries are crossed as administrators discover that their years of administrative practice have not provided them with the cultural knowledge necessary to effectively perform in cultural roles (Colon, 1991; Hayes, 1985; Jaschik, 1987; Siggelkow, 1991).

The cultural issues presently faced by student affairs administrators are more complex than those previously encountered. The level of cultural knowledge needed to survive as an administrator has significantly increased over the last several years (Altbach, 1991). Student issues are more difficult and often impossible to resolve without understanding the cultural differences of the students involved (Fellows, 1972). People of color have become empowered to such an extent that feelings of anger and frustration, expressed privately in the past, are no longer relegated to restricted settings. Administrators must seriously examine their level of multicultural expertise and skill in working with underrepresented groups. "Mere understanding will not solve all of America's racial and ethnic problems . . . but increased understanding is probably a step in the right direction for most of us" (Fellows, 1972, p. vii).

Cross-cultural counseling (Atkinson, Morten, and Sue, 1989; D. W. Sue and D. Sue, 1990; D. W. Sue, 1992) provides an ethical model for working with students from underrepresented groups. This model states that the counselor, prior to working with a client from a different ethnic or cultural group, *must* understand the dimensions of that client's circumstances. This understanding goes beyond cultural knowledge to include a demeanor that invites the client to share and grow without having to educate the counselor about cultural differences and similarities. Cross-cultural counselors cannot ethically place clients in the situation of having to educate them about cultural differences. The counselor must acquire the cross-cultural skills needed prior to entering a relationship with the client.

The ethics of cross-cultural counseling emanate from the belief that without cultural knowledge, the counselor may not recognize the client's problem, may underestimate the influence of racism on the client's life, and may not understand the nuances communicated by the client. A counselor seeking to conduct cross-cultural counseling has an ethical obligation to fully understand the background, language, and experiences of that client.

Conversely, student affairs administrators from the dominant culture are not guided by standards specifically related to cross-cultural administration. Through workshops, panel discussions, and individual conversations they often place students of color in the position of educating them about nondominant cultures. This stance not only unfairly burdens students who are struggling to pursue their academic goals but also perpetuates monocultural practices. Eurocentric culture is taught formally and informally throughout educational institutions whereas non-Eurocentric cultures are taught informally by the people representing those cultures (Aronowitz and Giroux, 1991; Botstein, 1991). In other words, Eurocentric cultural knowledge occupies privileged space within educational institutions, particularly in the curriculum, while non-Eurocentric knowledge is learned "on the streets" through nonprivileged means.

The student affairs educator as cultural broker must have multicultural knowledge so that he or she can broker or straddle the different cultures. A central concern of this straddling effort is ethnocentrism, or the inclination of all people to privilege their own culture over others. This occurs most readily when lack of knowledge about another's culture prevents the administrator from considering various behavioral styles that grow from a student's culture-related experiences. Examples include different conceptions of punctuality and communication styles (Astone and Nuñez-Wormack, 1990; Helgesen, 1990). Similar to the counselor, the administrator devoid of this cultural knowledge may fail to recognize the issue being raised by the student (for example, the importance of struggle in student activism; Marin, 1992), the leadership style that works for the student (for example, collaboration rather than competition; Locust, 1988), and the value that the student places on a particular issue (for example, family responsibility over leadership position; Arredondo, 1991).

The student affairs profession's long-standing goal of encouraging students to develop to their fullest potential (American Council on Education, 1937, 1949) entails multicultural skills and knowledge. Administrators who have not been trained in multiculturalism or undergone a reflexive process toward self-discovery cannot ethically be expected to teach race and culture classes, conduct cultural immersion workshops, offer programs in residence halls, or work effectively with students of color. But these same administrators cannot deny students of color their time and educational efforts. The need for equitable systems dictates that student affairs educators become multicultural administrators (Hayes, 1985).

Just as there are no easy ways to assess a student's knowledge of cultural issues, there are no easy ways to assess an administrator's level of expertise in multicultural issues. Self-assessment in particular is a dangerous practice. Rather than self-assessment, staff members should consider co-evaluation with a trusted, multiculturally aware colleague. Active participation in workshops and conferences is also helpful to self-assessment.

One of the essential aspects of multiculturalism is honest feedback. A primary means to assess one's skills concerning multiculturalism is through feedback from others. Student affairs educators must take down the barriers that prevent them from hearing the feedback that students provide about multiculturalism, including the feedback embedded in the backlash resulting from multicultural initiatives. Student affairs educators must understand students' concerns about these initiatives in order to make additional interventions effective. Although negative feedback is among the most difficult to obtain and to hear, it is most important to receive. Leadership in this regard means having the courage to open oneself to honest feedback as well as the willingness to change in response to this assessment.

Student Advocacy. Student advocacy is a traditional role (Appleton, Briggs, and Rhatigan, 1978) through which student affairs educators represent the student point of view to other campus administrators. This role creates a double-edged sword for student affairs educators who are charged with keeping student activism under control while encouraging student growth through personal decision making. The student advocacy role embodies contradictions in the ways that administrators attempt to achieve both of these goals. The task of "keeping the peace" may conflict with efforts to build students' confidence, integrity, and purpose (Chickering, 1969). This "peace" falls short of the reality of the fractious open dialogue necessary for student development and growth.

The student advocate role, always a complicated one for student affairs educators, takes on additional features of complexity when cross-cultural communication and understanding are introduced. A dominant culture vice president for student affairs working to express the needs of a black student union represents a different set of circumstances from the kind of student advocacy originally defined in predominantly white settings. Student affairs educators must redefine the traditional advocacy role to include cross-cultural relationships. The newly defined advocacy role should include constant self-examination in terms of multicultural attitudes, establishment of trusting relationships with students, educational efforts with upper administration, development of cross-cultural communication skills, and creation of opportunities for students to directly express their needs.

Ensure Optimum Performance

The next aspect of the cultural broker role is to empower students of color and majority students to ensure their optimum performance. A primary aspect of this goal is to remove the barriers that stand in the way of student achievement.

Trust. An essential aspect of ensuring optimal performance for all students is to trust them to understand their own needs. Mutual trust between students and administrators, as implicitly suggested in the cultural broker model, is unfortunately antithetical to traditional paternalistic administration.

Freire (1970) offers a way to view educator-student relationships that minimizes the distinction between the two roles. Freire assumes that both parties have a great deal to learn from each other. This learning, though, is often thwarted by differences in power between the student and the educator. Instead of being defined by that power, the educational experience in Freire's conception is defined by dialogue and collaboration between people who are simultaneously teacher-student and student-teacher. This stance decreases the artificial dualism that separates the educator from the student, and vice versa. It privileges both, rather than one person over the other, as people who have something to teach and learn.

The moral imperative inherent to multicultural action involves working together to understand the variety of perspectives that exists within any given situation. The administrator's and student's guard must be let down so that their vulnerabilities (for example, knowledge not known, mistakes made) are exposed. This approach flies in the face of pedagogical methods that emphasize control of the learning environment, one-way communication, students as tabulae rasae, and traditional student affairs professionalism.

Communication. Communication with students who seriously address issues of culture and ethnicity is essential to the creation of a multicultural environment. This open and honest dialogue is most important when it is most difficult. When dialogue seems impossible because of differences in opinion, power conflicts, and diverse cultural perspectives, administrators and students must find and create opportunities for the dialogue to continue. Although there are no guarantees of success, continued dialogue under the most adverse conditions can occur when all involved attempt to establish trusting relationships.

The path to these trusting relationships is difficult to follow, as many students involved in campus dissent do not fit the traditional profile of students chosen for or elected to student affairs paraprofessional staff and leadership positions. Success in building relationships with multicultural students, who are outside the bounds of traditional student affairs practice and theory, means understanding cultural perspectives different from those of the dominant culture. Students entering into a cross-cultural relationship with an administrator bring a perspective informed by racism and prejudice (D. W. Sue and D. Sue, 1991). As such, they are justifiably skeptical (D. W. Sue, 1992).

The role of struggle in achieving equity is an example of a multiculturally significant issue that student affairs administrators must understand as they craft close relationships with students of color (Marin, 1992). Nonviolent disruptive dissent (for example, arrests, sit-ins) is a well-established and accepted tactic within minority communities. The reasoning behind such struggle includes distrust of systems (represented by "the administration") that have failed and at times thwarted the efforts of people of color to achieve equity. An issue that a student of color may describe as struggle in the name of equity and social justice is often described by dominant culture administrators and students as disruption (Marin, 1992). It is important that student affairs educators bridge this misunderstanding gap as they seek nonviolent interventions during periods of racial unrest.

Take Action

Student affairs educators are pivotal actors in campus efforts directed toward multiculturalism and cross-cultural understanding. Indeed, the student affairs profession has historically been a vanguard for human rights issues on college campuses. Student affairs administrators, throughout the 1980s, accepted and were assigned responsibility for multicultural educational efforts. They took a holistic campus approach to the task. Although a holistic approach is necessary for long-range systemic change, student affairs administrators also need to recognize the progress being made in specific areas around campus. Pockets of understanding can be created by student affairs educators through efforts separate from institutionwide commitments. To be sure, multicultural efforts are not always understood or encouraged by all peoples across all areas of the institution. But lack of agreement, understanding, and commitment is not sufficient reason to cease efforts toward multiculturalism in a student affairs department or division. Pockets of understanding and multicultural staffs can form a cumulative grass-roots effort that catches the institution up in change toward multiculturalism.

Taking risks in the name of multicultural efforts is heart-wrenching work. But the ability to succeed at a task that requires passion and compassion can only be called leadership. It is leadership that invites dominant culture students to take responsibility to change their behavior, denounces hate crimes, calls attention to racist actions, and confronts ingrained attitudes.

Racial injustices are the daily events with which students of color have come to live. Student affairs administrators in cooperation and collaboration with students of color encourage institutional transformation to a multi-cultural environment by asking dominant culture students to condemn these injustices as well as adhere to a behavioral standard of civility and equality. This style of leadership is one that clearly states the goals and expectations about multiculturalism in a nonpaternalistic fashion. Leadership from administrators and educators can be exercised in ways that call social injustices to students' attention. By doing so, open and honest environments are created, and students are challenged to think more critically about their own actions and behaviors, those of their peers, and the standards that exist in the campus community. This leadership empowers dominant culture students to be more open and tolerant.

Summary

Students on many campuses are providing tremendous momentum and leadership in the movement toward multiculturalism. Students differ from administrators in their ability to see equity issues in ways unencumbered by traditional conventions of bureaucracies. Progress toward multiculturalism entails a cooperative effort between students and administrators. Students need their means of progressive action to be tempered with the maturity and organizational know-how of administrators. Administrators need to have their views of what is possible inspired by the idealism and insight of students. The collaboration of both can transform the institution into a multicultural environment.

Campus diversity is most obvious in the residence hall environment. Differences among students that may be interesting or stimulating in class or among friends can seem grating and tiresome in a roommate. Ways in which the cultural broker model can be helpful to residence hall staff are discussed.

The Cultural Broker in the Living Environment

No member of society escapes the strictures of conformity, whether in the home, classroom, social club, or as a member of an athletic team. While the lessons of our families' expectations of us may be long forgotten, most of us can remember aspects of an early, sometimes painful transition from "home" into a larger society with a different set of expectations. For most of us, those memories probably center around the first attendance at school (for a moving account of this transition by a Native American child, see Suina, 1988). Most typically, while undergoing this transition, each of us had a home to return to as a source of comfort, support, nurturing, and reassurance.

Students who move from home for the first time to attend college are making an abrupt transition in their home base. Each seeks in some way to recreate a semblance of home away from home. Some decorate with reminders of their hometown or high school, pictures of family and friends, or favorite pillows and stuffed animals. Others quickly identify social groups to replace family members and often the resident adviser becomes a surrogate mother or father.

One challenge in the transition to college is conformity to differences in expectations about roommates and floormates. Just as students are faced with the task of recreating home in an entirely new setting, they realize that those around them do not match preconceived notions about the "ideal roommate" or "the sibling I never had." Sometimes, this discrepancy is apparent with roommates whose own notions of home seem alien to the observers.

Early studies of the campus living environment demonstrated clearly the powerful pressures that result when students feel different from those around them (Brown, 1968; DeCoster, 1968). In these experimental studies, select students were assigned to residence halls so that they differed in some way from the majority of their floormates. In Brown's (1968) study, students were assigned so that 25 percent of them had one type of major and 75 percent had another (humanities versus sciences). In DeCoster's (1968) study, low-achievement students were assigned to a floor with a large percentage of high-achieving floormates, and vice versa. The evidence pointed to an underlying pressure to conform. In both studies, students who were "outnumbered" typically changed. Outnumbered humanities majors changed to science majors; outnumbered science majors changed to humanities majors. Low achievers rose to the occasion and became higher achievers; high achievers who were outnumbered achieved less than expected. Additionally, the few who did not "conform" felt dissatisfied with their experience.

These results, indicating change in the face of the strong pressure that students feel when they differ from their peers, demonstrate a phenomenon known as *progressive conformity*. The notion of progressive conformity could be extended logically to the kinds of pressures that new students feel, particularly those who differ from the mainstream culture in an institution. Some of these students might find themselves changing or "assimilating" to a culture that is not really their own, one that is "prescribed" by the majority of the students with whom they live. Other students, who resist the pressures of progressive conformity, like the numerical minority of students in the studies described above, might feel less satisfied with their college experience.

Probably nowhere on campus is diversity more obvious than in the residence hall environment. Differences among students that may be interesting or stimulating in class or among friends can seem grating and tiresome in a roommate. Residence hall staff, including resident assistants (RAs), have a responsibility to be aware and understanding of each student whom they serve. The relationship between the individual and the environment must be comfortable if he or she is to achieve maximum growth and development (Banning, 1989). In this chapter, the term *multicultural students* refers primarily to members of ethnic, racial, and cultural groups, but the ideas presented here could be extended to women; returning students; gay, lesbian, and bisexual students; first-generation students; and others who are not a part of the dominant culture.

This chapter presents the cultural broker model as a means of encouraging cultural pluralism in the living environment. Models of identity development are examined as a way of viewing the challenges to multiculturalism that are presented by group living. The role of the residence life administrator as cultural broker is discussed, and the model is presented as a framework for educating residence hall staff. Finally, a vignette from Chapter One is reexamined from the cultural broker perspective.

Identity Development of Students in Residence Halls

Recently, many ethnic identity development and multicultural awareness models have appeared (or reappeared) in the student affairs and counseling literatures (Atkinson, Morten, and Sue, 1989; M. Bennett, 1986; Cass, 1984; Helms, 1984; D. W. Sue and D. Sue, 1985). These models are useful for those seeking to understand and appreciate others on a diverse campus and may be particularly useful for residence hall staff. Space limitations permit discussion of only two models here (see Moore, 1990, particularly W. Jones, 1990, for a discussion of a wide range of identity development models; also see Evans and Wall, 1991, for identity development models of gay, lesbian, and bisexual students).

Atkinson, Morten, and Sue's (1989) model of minority identity development (MID) is useful for understanding the development of a broad range of ethnically diverse students. Additionally, principles of the model can be extended to other individuals who are outside the mainstream of campus culture. The model suggests five stages or transitions that represent development of awareness of one's own and others' cultures: conformity, dissonance, resistance and immersion, introspection, and synergistic articulation and awareness.

The first stage, conformity, describes an ethnic minority who demonstrates a preference for and identity with the dominant culture. An individual at this stage may not feel an affiliation or sense of identity with other members of his or her own culture or ethnic group and may avoid them. An example is an African American woman who socializes and eats with only majority women on her floor. She usually does not invite her roommate, who also happens to be African American, to join them. During sorority rush, she avoids the African American sororities' parties.

Individuals experiencing the dissonance stage demonstrate an increasing awareness of their own culture. They begin to feel conflict and confusion over who they are and what is important to them. An individual at this stage might include a gay male who begins to realize the source of discomfort that he feels at residence hall social events. Because most of these events focus on heterosexual dating activities, when he attends, he feels like he is misrepresenting himself to women who seem interested in him. He also feels conflict as well as betrayal over the "gay bashing" common to residence hall life.

Students in the resistance-and-immersion stage may be the most challenging for student affairs staff. This stage is characterized by complete rejection of the dominant culture, complete acceptance of one's own culture, and relative indifference to and unawareness of other minority cultures. An example might be a woman who has recently discovered feminism. She takes only courses cross-listed with women's studies, is quick to point out instances of "sexism" on campus, and, more than once, has contributed to the disruption of meetings by accusing others of being "sexist pigs."

The introspection stage is characterized by feelings of conflict over the absolutes experienced during the resistance-and-immersion stage. Here, the individual becomes more aware of the relative merits of individuals regardless of culture. The resolution of conflicts experienced during the introspection stage leads to the final stage, synergistic articulation and awareness. This stage is characterized by selective appreciation of aspects of one's own, the dominant, and other minority cultures. A student in these later stages of the model might include the former president of the Latino Student Association. He serves on the Residence Life Multicultural Awareness Board and helps with multicultural awareness training throughout campus.

Atkinson, Morten, and Sue (1989) acknowledge that it is not necessary for individuals to pass through each stage of the model. Rather, they present the model for counselors as a way of promoting understanding and guiding the development of those who are struggling in the campus environment.

Helms's (1984) model describes the development of white racial identity. This model also has five stages: contact, disintegration, reintegration, pseudo-independence, and autonomy. The first stage, contact, is characterized by minimal awareness of the existence of minority groups and no concept of one's own race. This stage includes many students who experience their first interethnic contacts when they go to college. A student at this stage might include the majority student, Rob, described in the third vignette of Chapter One. Rob's parents objected to his African American roommate. Rob quickly made friends with other majority students on the floor and made no effort to get to know his roommate.

The second stage, disintegration, entails acknowledgment of prejudice and discrimination, and accumulation of knowledge about one's own race. Persons at this stage might include students who attend a first-year seminar that includes a diversity unit or who attend a multicultural workshop in their residence hall.

At the reintegration stage, a majority individual blames minority group members for creating their own problems. This stage could include students who say, "If blacks want to be accepted for themselves, they should go to a historically black college—otherwise, adapt." It also might include students who wonder why diverse students are given special "privileges" such as Latino cultural centers and African American student unions.

At the pseudo-independence stage comes conscious acceptance of other ethnic groups and interest in understanding racial and cultural differences. This stage includes residence hall student leaders and RAs who work to promote racial understanding. Finally, at the autonomy stage the individual exhibits growing knowledge about racial and cultural similarities and appreciation of all cultures.

While these two models have been criticized for placing people in categories or for being too linear, they provide useful conceptualizations of very complex problems. For example, a RA happens upon two of his African

American residents violating the noise policy during finals week. Knowledge of the MID model (Atkinson, Morten, and Sue, 1989) may be helpful to the RA when the two students call him a racist as he writes up their violation. The feeling that much of the dominant institution is racist, sexist, or homophobic may be part of a minority student's immersion into his or her own culture and development of new knowledge about social inequities (MID, Stage 3). The RA could let the students know about his part in numerous other, similar incidents in the past month involving majority students, talk to them about some of the work that he personally has done to promote pluralism, and let them know how being called a "racist" makes him feel. While he probably will not see evidence of changes in the students' attitudes, his efforts to communicate his own perspective could spark feelings of dissonance in a student who has otherwise gotten along well with the RA and who is ready to move to a higher stage of identity development. Communication of his perspective is also a rational response by the RA, who might feel enraged at the accusation of racism.

It is important that education of residence hall staff include presentation of theoretical models on which to base problem interventions. The importance of the education of residence hall staff is widely accepted within the student affairs profession (Stage, Schuh, Hosler, and Westfall, 1991; Winston and Ender, 1988). In an effort to address problems associated with diversity issues, most residence hall systems have instituted workshops and encounters among and between diverse staff and residents. VanBebber (1991) describes some excellent techniques for integrating diversity into hall staff courses.

However, residence hall educational programs, while useful in introducing people to the seriousness of the issues involved, sometimes fall short of what is needed to truly change residence hall climates. Often, the programs resemble "cultures on display" (Leppo, 1987), with inadequate time spent delving beyond surface issues. Years of effort have demonstrated that cultural pluralism cannot easily be programmed. What is needed is a systematic and continuous process for changing individual perspectives that moves beyond mere awareness of issues and toward empathic understanding (Manning and Coleman-Boatwright, 1991). The cultural broker model can serve as a guide for a dynamic process of change. It is something that can be taken beyond the workshop and into everyday staff meetings, judicial conferences, and social activities.

Residence Hall Staff as Cultural Brokers

The cultural broker model, as earlier described, encompasses four components: learning to think contextually, boundary spanning, ensuring optimum performance, and taking action. As a first step, in learning to think contextually, residence hall staff begin to recognize and understand various cultures within their college, particularly within their own residence hall setting. In their work with diverse students, their job is to learn about many cultures, not to teach diverse students to assimilate into the majority culture.

The second part of the cultural broker model requires those working with students in residence life to enter new worlds. The challenge here is to experiment with language, notions of time, and ways of enjoying oneself. The staff member learns to be comfortable and enjoy settings other than the most familiar. This learning might include exploration of new areas of creativity, participation in social events that are unfamiliar, and acquisition of knowledge from individuals in the residence hall.

In the third step of the model, residence hall staff seek to ensure optimal performance for all students. The work here includes helping students to refine their skills and allowing avenues for expression of all students' talents. Residence life staff can discourage overparticipation by a few enthusiastic students to provide for a broader spectrum of participation by many.

Finally, the cultural broker becomes an activist in his or her residence hall and on the campus. Because most campus staff members' resources are stretched, the cultural broker should, when necessary, be selective about participation on committees and governance structures. The broker should choose activities that are likely to have the greatest impact on the lives of diverse students and the greatest influence on the campus community.

A Cultural Broker Model Workshop for Staff and Students

The cultural broker model provides an ideal framework for extending responsibility for pluralism to those working (hall staff, RAs, and student leaders) and living within the residence hall environment. Workshops for these groups can begin to move individuals through early steps of the model and also guide the work of the later stages. Although a single workshop is insufficient to fully develop an individual as a cultural broker, movement through the components of the model within the "safe" context of the workshop can create guidelines for later behaviors.

In the early stages of the workshop, for example, staff members could view prewritten vignettes staged by other members of the residence life staff. The vignettes would be designed to represent actual situational conflicts resulting from diversity within residence halls. Viewers would then be asked to write anonymously about their reactions to individual characters in the vignettes, and the reactions would be turned in to the workshop facilitator. After a break, the facilitator would choose some of the reactions for discussion. Some of the reactions may reflect an unfavorable view of a character in one of the vignettes. The facilitator would present those perspectives along with opposing perspectives that reflect a more favorable view of the character. These alternative perspectives may be contained in other viewers' anonymous responses, or they may be thought out ahead of time by the facilitator.

For example, one vignette might include a white student, Estelle, who complains about her Latino American roommate, Lila. She gets along with Lila; however, as soon as Lila's friends come in, she begins speaking Spanish. Estelle feels left out and says that when they all laugh, they look at her, making her feel uncomfortable in her own room. When they are there, she cannot study and she cannot participate in their fun either.

A workshop participant may view Lila as selfish or uncaring. Another perspective may view Lila's interaction with her friends as natural for those whose second language is English. A visit with her friends gives Lila an opportunity to relax and not have to worry about translations. Some workshop participants, in their reactions to Estelle, may describe her as jealous or insecure. Others may understand that it is normal for someone to feel left out when in the company of those who are speaking another language.

In the next stage of the workshop participants would role-play the parts of Lila and Estelle, and the facilitator would play the part of the RA helping the students enjoy and learn from one another. Parts could be chosen so that participants sympathetic to particular characters would play those roles.

Other plots for vignettes might include harassment of African American students by dominant culture residents when the black students host an annual dance in a residence hall facility, problems with eye contact and communication between Asian American and Euroamerican roommates, and living style differences between a white and African American roommate. For example, a white student may complain that the roommate's hair dressing smells, that he plays music loudly, and that he has friends over who sit on both beds. Another might include white students who complain that other students on campus get special privileges such as the Black Student Union, the International Student Center, the Commuter Student Lounge, and the Latino Cultural Festival; they want to know when they will have their own special events or space.

Conclusion

In Chapter One, we presented a vignette about a black student, Dave, who has racial problems with his white roommate, Rob. In that vignette, the administrator, Waters, made certain assumptions that led to a denial of Dave's request for a new roommate. Her reasons for the denial included that she did not want to convey mixed messages to the campus community and that she thought that Rob might learn something from the experience.

Rethinking the scenario from the cultural broker perspective, Waters would stop to consider the perspective of the black student in this campus situation. As a new student who is not part of the dominant culture, what kinds of supports does he have as opposed to the dominant culture student? What kind of situation is Dave placed in when he is required to educate others? Who should change his behavior in this situation, Dave or Rob, or both?

In an idealistic reconsideration of this fictional scenario, Residence Life Director Waters would consider the possibility that Rob's hostility puts undue emotional stress on Dave while he is dealing with the typical, new student adjustments to college. She considers modifying the residence life policy. Dave, the African American student, is allowed to room with a friend that he has made on the floor. She reconsiders the notion of what's good for the majority in balance with what is good for the multicultural student. She decides to explore suggestions that residence life allow diverse students to choose between a mainstream room assignment and a residence hall with a concentration of diverse students. Of course, such decisions may be controversial. Waters must be prepared to defend her actions by demonstrating that a hostile roommate would be detrimental to Dave's success as a college student.

The residence hall living unit is an important focus for the student undergoing a transition into a new college environment. Residence hall staff can play an important role in this transition. As Schlossberg's (1989) concepts of "marginality" and "mattering" serve to clarify, the transition to college provides a perfect setting for a student to feel marginal. If, during that transition period, the student gradually comes to feel important to the college community, to feel that he or she "matters," then the transition to college is a success. If, on the other hand, a student continues to feel marginal, as if living life within two distinct cultures, his or her own as well as that of the campus culture, never feeling quite accepted, then the transition is a failure.

The degree to which administrators can create open and flexible environments in the residence halls will determine their success as cultural brokers. The hall environment must be inclusive, that is, accepting of differences among individuals so that each student is appreciated for his or her own unique contributions to the residential community. All students must know that they matter.

The cocurriculum includes any activity that takes place outside the college classroom. While this spectrum is so broad that it offers great challenge to the cultural broker, it also offers opportunities for creating a multicultural campus.

The Cultural Broker and the Cocurriculum

Many important experiences contributing to college students' development occur outside the classroom. The well-known Tinto (1975) model of college student persistence has formed a basis for nearly two decades of research on college students' success and satisfaction. The social integration of the student on campus is one of two major dimensions of that model (academic integration is the other). Researchers have found elements of the social dimension of campus life to be as important as academic elements in influencing educational success for some groups of college students (Nora and Rendon, 1990; Pascarella, 1985; Stage, 1989b).

Additionally, other theories of college student growth and development posit strong links between student activities and campus involvement and classroom and educational success. These theories include Pace's (1979, 1988) work with the College Student Experiences Questionnaire, Astin's (1985) theory of involvement, Leafgren's (1986) work on wellness and campus recreation, and Bloland's (1987) view of leisure as a source for fostering student development. Pascarella and Terenzini's (1991) review of twenty years of research on college students concludes that student extra-curricular involvement has at least a modest, positive, postcollege influence on career achievement. Additionally, Manning (1989) and Schlossberg (1989) write about the importance of campus rituals and activities for creating a sense of belonging for students.

These cocurricular activities on the campus can be defined as anything that takes place outside the formal classroom. An alternative definition might be any college experience that is not recorded on a student's transcript. However, a few campuses, such as Alverno College (Mentkowski and Doherty, 1984) recognize the importance of cocurricular experiences and do record at least some of them on transcripts.

The cocurriculum on the college campus includes clubs, organizations, and other, similar student activities; student governance; intramural and informal sports organizations; social activities; art, literary, and musical experiences; and jobs and internship opportunities. Whether students are engaged in these activities as active participants or as passive observers, the cocurriculum flavors their lives.

Lloyd-Jones (1989) reminded us of the student personnel concept (as old as 1937) that campus recreation and activities are important to the growth and development of college students. Indeed, organized campus activities could be viewed as a college's attempt to manage the cocurriculum of college students. Today, management of those activities involves a major commitment of personnel and funds from student affairs divisions. It also comprises shares of the budgets of schools of health, physical education, and recreation, music departments, and fine arts departments, demonstrating administrators' belief in the importance of the cocurriculum. On most campuses, the importance of activities and recreation in students' lives outside the classroom is unquestioned.

While there is only a smattering of research focusing on the effectiveness of programs and activities specifically designed for minority students (Harris, 1991; Sedlacek, 1987), it is assumed that these programs too are important. Unfortunately, on many college campuses, the model for participation in student activities is either assimilation into the dominant group's activities or separation and creation of new activities marginal to the mainstream of campus life (Chavez and Carlson, 1986; Manning, 1988; Ringgenberg, 1989). It is difficult to find a campus that is truly integrated in its student activities. It is even more difficult to find a campus where large numbers of students of the dominant culture feel free to participate in diverse student organizations and activities and where the majority of diverse students are active participants in mainstream activities.

In Chapter Two, the cultural broker model was presented as a way of creating a multicultural campus environment. The components of the model—learning to think contextually, boundary spanning, ensuring optimal performance, and taking action—can guide those who work with college students outside the classroom in efforts to value and foster diversity on their campus. In this chapter, the term *multicultural students* refers primarily to members of ethnically diverse students, but the ideas presented here could also be extended to women; returning students; gay, lesbian, and bisexual students; first-generation students; and others who are not a part of the mainstream. The purpose of this chapter is to discuss the campus activity planner's role as a cultural broker. First, we discuss a variety of elements of the cocurriculum, as well as possible barriers to diverse students' participation in cocurricular activities. Then we present a model of program planning described in terms of the cultural broker model.

The Cocurriculum on a Diverse Campus

Ideally, the cocurriculum on a college campus serves all students. The development and planning of activities today are no longer based on the notion that each campus activity can, if properly designed, involve and meet the needs of all students. It is now realized that this all-encompassing goal is unattainable, that no one activity or group of activities can ever meet all students' needs, even on a relatively small, homogeneous campus. Current college campuses present their students with smorgasbords of activities, events, and programs in efforts to provide as many choices to as many students as possible.

Despite this change in strategy, there is still room for evolution in the planning of student activities. Consider the following ways that our campuses could provide even more choice and inclusion in their activities planning: (1) An intramural program could allow interested groups to design and organize their own competition. For example, Southeast Asian students could hold a sepaktakraw tournament (a game similar to badminton but played by kicking a wicker ball). Teams could be organized to include players from two groups, experienced players as well as interested learners. An exhibition game with master players might also be part of the activity. (2) A campus activities planning and funding process could include broader input. For example, a student activities board could dedicate one-quarter of its funding to activities that are selected through invited proposals from the campus community at large. (3) Cultural activities and programs could remove barriers to student participation. For example, campus musical groups could allow students to participate without registering for extra courses, committing to excessive practice times, or otherwise jeopardizing their academic commitments. As a second example, campus-based artist cooperatives could provide studio space during off hours for students who are not majors but for whom artistic expression is an important aspect of their lives.

Administrators of campus activities and programs must seek new ways of providing their services, ways in which they can continuously seek input from students, especially those who are least represented in the current planning structures. Jacoby (1991) writes of the diversity of students who must be served by student affairs functions. In particular, she points to Cross's (1981) classification of perceived barriers to adult participation in higher education: situational, dispositional, and institutional. This classification can be extended to the barriers that limit diverse student participation in campus activities. Situational barriers might include lack of time or monetary resources that prevents participation in certain kinds of activities. Another situational barrier for some students could be opposition or lack of support from peers. Dispositional barriers for diverse students might include lack of confidence in themselves and their abilities, lack of knowledge about campus programs and services, and feelings of being unwelcome or an outsider. Finally, institutional barriers could be confronted by diverse students when programs cater to the needs and interests of one particular kind of student to the exclusion of others.

Student affairs administrators and, indeed, higher education institutions must assume responsibility for eliminating these barriers. Situational barriers, especially activities that require monetary resources and thus separate the "haves" from the "have not's," should be prime targets. For example, an annual spring weekend that includes a concert, sports activity, and dinner-dance for $75 a couple is a situational barrier to many students. Low-income students attending college primarily on financial aid probably will not attend this campuswide "Rites of Spring Celebration." However, by selling low-cost "work-celebrate" tickets, a broader array of students can be included in the event.

A common dispositional barrier to student participation in campus services and activities is a lack of knowledge about them. On most campuses, strides have been made to ensure that all students know about services provided throughout campus. On some campuses, however, activities are publicized through the school paper, which is often a subscription paper. An advertisement publicizing an impending deadline for soccer team signups might be missed by international students who have not been provided money for the student paper in their allotted budgets. By posting an announcement in residence halls where international students reside, or at an office for international students, administrators might overcome this dispositional barrier.

Institutional barriers occur when needs and interests of only one kind of student are considered in the design of activities. Much work has been done recently to remove these barriers. However, because many activities and programs are deeply ingrained in our institutions (for example, homecoming, traditional intramural sports), they are not easily altered. Indeed, on some campuses, traditional activities absorb so much of the extracurricular programming budget that attempts to broaden offerings or to include more diverse students end up as token efforts at best.

Manning's (1988) model presents a range of ways of incorporating diverse students into the mainstream of campus activities. At the lowest levels of the model, the activities planners have a monocultural view of the world. Activities and programs reflect only the tastes and values of the dominant culture students on campus. At the middle levels of the model, more diverse cultural planning is included in activities and programs, but only in token ways—an African American history week here, a cultural festival there. The remainder of the year's activities reflects a monocultural worldview. Finally, at the highest levels of the model, multicultural programs and events, with cooperation, recommendations, and participation of diverse students and staff, are presented throughout the year. Manning's model could be used to critically review program planning at institutions. What level of multicultural programming currently exists on the campus? If the answer is lower or middle levels according to the model, a reexamination of the program planning process is probably in order.

The Cultural Broker Model and Program Planning

Program and activity planning is an important means for creating a diverse cocurricular environment. Program planning has been discussed extensively in the literature (for example, Moore and Delworth, 1976; Morrill, 1989). Russell (1982) presents a straightforward planning model. Since it includes steps contained in most planning models, it is used here to demonstrate implementation of the cultural broker model on campus. The components of the planning model include needs assessment, determination of objectives, generation of program and activity possibilities, development of the program, implementation, and evaluation.

The first stage in the planning process, needs assessment, is the most familiar to those planning programs and activities, but that familiarity makes it the most dangerous stage. The danger is that program planners will mistakenly assume that it is sufficient to conduct another survey or, worse, a casual interview of interested parties. In order to truly meet diverse needs at this phase of the planning process, one must make an effort to reach multicultural students, whether by attending meetings of special student groups, forming an advisory council of leaders of diverse organizations, or targeting surveys to particular groups of students in addition to a general distribution.

The design of the needs assessment also should not be taken for granted. A list of multiple-choice questions about recreational interests merely reflects the experiences and opinions of the person or persons designing the questionnaire. A thorough needs assessment includes other methods for eliciting thoughts, opinions, and new ideas. Analysis of attendance at past meetings and events, nonreactive measures, interviews, and focus groups are just a few of the methods that could be used to generate information (for a description of diverse methods for conducting needs assessments, see Stage, 1992b).

The second stage, determination of objectives of the program or programs, involves analysis and interpretation of the needs assessment. For this stage of planning, the student affairs administrator is usually working with a committee or division in determining goals for the cocurriculum based on the needs revealed in the first step. As cultural brokers, student affairs staff seek to incorporate diverse programs and activities throughout the year. They also seek to meet the needs of diverse groups and individuals identified through the targeted needs assessment. Possible objectives for a committee seeking diversity in their offerings might include a program that is *inclusive* of all students on campus, a program that is *responsive* to students' expressed needs throughout the year, and a program that *actively* recruits diverse students on campus to participate in activities.

The third step, generation of program and activity possibilities, is the most creative part of the process. This step could include a brainstorming session that focuses separately on each of the objectives generated in the second stage. The session could begin with an activity designed to stimulate creative thinking in a group. Warmup exercises can be found in many books on creativity or brainstorming available in most public libraries. The session should also focus on extant programs and activities and consider modifications, eliminations, or expansions. This stage of the process must include input from multicultural staff and students, especially leaders of diverse student groups. At this point, the brainstorming should include all possibilities, ignoring for the moment cost and other constraints.

For the next step, development of the program, cost and other constraints ignored earlier must now be considered. One can aid the decision making at this step by creating a matrix of program objectives by cost: high, medium, or low. Ideas from the brainstorming sessions of the previous stage are then placed in the appropriate cells of the matrix. Table 7.1 is a hypothetical matrix for development of a programming plan. For example, for the responsive program objective, a low-cost strategy might involve reallocation of part of a regular activities budget. A proportion could be

Table 7.1. Hypothetical Matrix for Multicultural Programming Decisions

| Objectives | Cost | | |
	Low	Medium	High
Inclusive	Continued encouragement student involvement in all activities	Funds for co-sponsorship of programs by dominant and diverse organizations	Provision of houses or clubs for all multicultural student groups
Responsive	Avenues for proposed programs within the regular budget	A few special programs based on ad hoc requests	New budget to meet program and activity requests
Proactive	Fliers and ads specifically aimed at diverse students	Creation of a weekly network of events for distribution to student leaders	"Scholarships" for diverse students to attend special campus events

provided for activities and programs proposed by college students at large. A medium-cost strategy might involve the allocation of new dollars to be held by a programming committee for response to ad hoc requests for programs and activities. Finally, a high-cost strategy (in the best of all possible worlds) might involve new allocation of funds to meet all requests for diverse programming.

A key task for the fifth stage, implementation, is to ensure that those active in the production of a program understand the objectives. Additionally, for student affairs administrators to be true cultural brokers, they must regularly attend the events that result from the multicultural planning and programming.

The final step in the loop, evaluation, is critical to the process but is most easily forgotten. While we are congratulating ourselves on a job well done, we may be missing the evaluations of others. One university programming board invited a well-known black South African musical group to perform on campus. The concert was well attended and included many multicultural faculty and administrators, but the audience was predominantly composed of white students. A visual survey of the audience revealed that the Black Student Union's leadership team was not in attendance. Later, it was learned that some of the musical group's politics in regard to apartheid were questionable. The planners had made assumptions about the kind of entertainment that the African American students on their campus would like. Ideally, that information would have been solicited from African American students and given to the planners of the event early in the process. Clearly, the incident demonstrates a weakness in the planning process that should be addressed the next time an event is planned.

An effective evaluation process provides program designers with the kind of information needed to correct planning deficiencies. This step in the process is very similar to the needs assessment step. Evaluation, to be useful, requires a broad range of respondents and a wide latitude of possible responses. It is critical to include nonparticipants as well as participants in the evaluation phase of a program.

Summary

In Chapter One, a scenario involving Student Activities Director Williams was discussed. In that vignette, Williams prided himself that his advisory style "allowed" student leadership to flourish. Under his mode of operation, students made their own decisions about budget allocations without benefit of his perspective.

Rethinking the scenario as a cultural broker, Williams would recognize his obligation to point out a perspective missing from the student senate's assessment of the Gay, Lesbian, and Bisexual Alliance funding request. Using totals, generated from student activities fees assessed from all students,

Williams would share findings indicating the amount of money allocated to predominantly white groups, the number of events planned for majority culture students, and the level of dissatisfaction with campus activities among students from diverse racial and ethnic groups. For example, students who are openly gay, lesbian, or bisexual may have indicated their extreme displeasure at the lack of support provided to the so-called alternative groups. When this information is shared with the student senate, they can discuss whether they have sufficiently recognized the full range of students on campus. During the discussion, it may be revealed that many leaders on the student senate support the Alliance but were pressured into silence by the conservative opinions of more vocal members of the senate. Williams is able to facilitate this honest sharing because of private discussions he has held with these previously silent students. The senate is particularly alarmed because they have prided themselves on the resolutions recently passed committing their group to the goals of multiculturalism. Discussion ensues, reconsidering the Gay, Lesbian, and Bisexual Alliance funding request. A task force, with a diverse representation from various campus groups, is assembled to rewrite the senate's funding policies. A more equitable system and an action-oriented commitment to cultural pluralism are the goals.

It is clear that in order to include diverse students in the programs and activities available on campus, we must move beyond a passive approach that "allows" students to participate. While it is important to offer the opportunity to participate, in order to be truly inclusive, all students must feel that they have been actively recruited to participate. By engaging in active efforts to involve all students, we can overcome barriers to student involvement in the campus community.

Finally, if the program planning process is to work as a cultural broker process, it must be repeated continuously. New information must continuously be sought, needs reassessed, goals set, programs designed and implemented, and, finally, evaluated again. Only when the program planning process is as dynamic as the student body on our campuses do we have a chance of meeting students' activity needs.

This chapter summarizes the key elements of the cultural broker perspective and presents a vision of the multicultural campus as we move toward the next century. An annotated bibliography of related works follows the chapter.

A Vision of the Multicultural Campus

Chapter One describes in detail actual situations confronted by those who work with college students on today's multicultural campuses. In Chapter Two, cultural brokering was presented as a model for flexibility and choice on the college campus. The elements of the model—learning to think contextually, spanning boundaries, ensuring optimal performance, and taking action—were presented as ways of viewing the role of student affairs educators in their work with diverse students. In the first step, as the cultural broker learns to think contextually, he or she begins to recognize the culture effused throughout the campus. The cultural broker also learns to recognize instances when cultural expectations and assumptions create dissonance for individual students.

In the second stage, boundary spanning, the student affairs educator becomes agile at moving into previously unfamiliar realms. With students and other diverse staff members as "hosts," he or she becomes increasingly familiar with a broad array of cultures. Ultimately, this experience reflects, in a small way, the experiences of ethnic minority students and others who are not part of the mainstream and who span cultural boundaries daily.

In the third stage, the broker uses the lessons learned from boundary spanning to change assumptions and broaden expectations of acceptable ways of being on campus. At this stage, the broker works with individual students to optimize their own strengths within the college through adaptation rather than assimilation.

Finally, in the fourth stage, the cultural broker takes action and becomes a leader, demonstrating ways of creating choice and options in campus communities. The model is viewed as dynamic in that there is no end of opportunity for a leader to span new boundaries, no reason that a boundary spanner, while learning, cannot lead others to create options and choices in the learning environment.

Later chapters described how administrative staff in various units of a college or university might apply the model in their own unique situations. The vignettes presented in Chapter One were re-resolved in later chapters with a vision of a multicultural campus that was populated or staffed by "cultural brokers."

These vignettes, involving culturally diverse students, represent challenging diversity issues that have become commonplace on most college campuses. Even as we developed what we thought were tough issues, tougher issues surfaced almost daily: displays of neo-Naziism on campus, free speech versus "political correctness" debates, harassment of ethnically diverse students by Eurocentric students, and gay, lesbian, and bisexual students demanding rights within the halls of academe that they do not have within society in general. At first, it was tempting to update our scenarios, to get the most recent *Chronicle of Higher Education* headline down on paper. We elected instead to let our model chase the headlines. The model evolved even as we wrote the book, so that finally we were satisfied that it was dynamic enough to grow and expand as all of us grow and expand in our capacity as cultural brokers.

While this book focuses on the real, hard issues in day-to-day life on college campuses, there are other issues that are nearly as important. Much of what we know about college students comes from research that has been conducted in this century. As we close on a century of research on college students, we see that new ways of knowing are becoming more important. Much of the past research focused on mean scores, trends, and predictions based on the ways that the majority of students behave. Unfortunately, that research does not tell us much about the 10 or 20 percent of students who do not fall within that majority. Fortunately, this problem has been recognized and researchers are beginning to make changes.

Student affairs educators, as consumers of research on college students, are in a position to help guide the research of the future. New questions, more difficult to answer, should be the future focus of research. Who are the students on our campuses (beyond demographic characterizations)? What would the ideal campus look like from a particular student's perspective? How does it look now? Do our classrooms provide optimal environments for each student to achieve to his or her capacity?

In addition to asking new questions, student affairs educators must also be open to new ways of viewing old questions. An optimal vision of the near future includes student affairs journals and books with articles that will help us as we learn to think contextually, span boundaries, ensure optimal performance, and take action.

Recall the image from Chapter One of the student affairs educator as border crosser, moving from one cultural situation to another, seeing similarity and difference, adapting style to situation, delving openly and readily into the unknown. In the re-resolutions of the scenarios described in the middle chapters of this volume, the educators involved reversed their decisions. In doing so, these administrators did not lose any of their decision-making power; rather, they used their authority, their knowledge, and their experience to empower others. Avenues were opened for possibilities that fit these peoples' professional agendas. No one gave up their ideals; they just broadened their perspectives. This sort of expansiveness shapes new behaviors, broadens one's own and others' perspectives, and enriches college life. This is the stuff of cultural brokerage.

ANNOTATED BIBLIOGRAPHY

The authors of this volume were influenced by a substantial body of literature on diverse students as well as diversity issues. References at the end of this book are a list of those influences. Here, we annotate the dozen or so works that had the greatest influence on us and that we found most inspiring.

Altbach, P. G., and Lomotey, K. *The Racial Crisis in American Higher Education.* Albany: State University of New York Press, 1991.
This edited work summarizes the debates and tensions that exist on college campuses on the issue of cultural pluralism. Chapter authors include educators who are well known for their role in fostering diversity on their campuses.

Atkinson, D. R., Morten, G., and Sue, D. W. *Counseling American Minorities: A Cross-Cultural Perspective.* (3rd ed.) Dubuque, Iowa: Brown, 1989.
The authors discuss cross-cultural issues from a counseling perspective. The first three chapters provide an insightful discussion of problematic words used to describe diverse populations. The minority identity development model is presented, and specific cultural groups are discussed.

Cheatham, H. E. (ed.). *Cultural Pluralism on Campus.* Alexandria, Va.: American College Personnel Association Media, 1991.
This volume addresses ways of creating a culturally pluralistic environment on the college campus. The book begins with chapters on the current state of diversity issues and affirmative action on campus. Subsequent chapters focus on specific issues of student affairs functional areas.

Evans, N. J., and Wall, V. A. *Beyond Tolerance: Gays, Lesbians, and Bisexuals on Campus.* Alexandria, Va.: American College Personnel Association Media, 1991.
This volume focuses on sexual orientation issues on the college campus. It is one of the few books available that pulls together literature on this particular topic.

Fleming, J. *Blacks in College: A Comparative Study of Students' Success in Black and White Institutions.* San Francisco: Jossey-Bass, 1984.
This landmark research on African American students covers the experiences of over one thousand students at seven colleges and universities. Students' experiences at predominantly black and predominantly white institutions are compared, and recommendations are provided for optimizing the campus environment.

Freire, P. *Pedagogy of the Oppressed.* New York: Continuum, 1970.
This classic work on cultural pluralism and oppression is required reading for all educators seeking to gain a broad understanding of the political, economic, and power relationships among people.

Helms, J. E. (ed.). *Black and White Racial Identity: Theory, Research, and Practice.* New York: Greenwood, 1991.
This book is a complete collection of both white and black racial identity models. Helms's work on white identity models, in particular, points the way to an antiracist agenda for college administrators.

Moore, L. V. (ed.). *Evolving Theoretical Perspectives on Students.* New Directions for Student Services, no. 51. San Francisco: Jossey-Bass, 1990.
This volume discusses student development theory in relation to diverse population groups. Chapters include discussion of theoretical models relative to gender differences, age differences, sexual orientation, and ethnicity. The authors present useful, refreshing, and inspiring new ways of looking at old theories.

Olivas, M. A. (ed.). *Latino College Students.* New York: Teachers College Press, 1986.
This book provides a theoretical review of the literature on Latino college students' educational attainment and college experiences. Most of the chapters are quantitatively based research studies of students on college campuses. Recommendations for expanding our knowledge of these students are provided.

Sagaria, M.A.D. (ed.). *Empowering Women: Leadership Development Strategies on Campus.* New Directions for Student Services, no. 44. San Francisco: Jossey-Bass, 1988.
This volume focuses on the development of leadership in college women. However, the generative leadership model presented by the editor could be extended to any student who falls outside the mainstream culture predominant on a campus.

Stage, F. K. (ed.). *Diverse Methods for Research and Assessment of College Students.* Alexandria, Va.: American College Personnel Association Media, 1992.
This book is a valuable resource for those who design and conduct research on or assessments of college students. The authors present arguments for diversifying ways of studying college students and their campus experiences—ways that ask new questions and expand possibilities for new learning.

Tierney, W. G. "The College Experience of Native Americans: A Critical Analysis." In L. Weis and M. Fine (eds.), *Silenced Voices: Issues of Class, Race, and Gender in Today's Schools.* Albany: State University of New York Press, 1991.
This inspiring chapter discusses the experiences of Native American students in higher education. The author uses the term "border crossers" to describe students who move from their own cultures to dominant campus culture. Our conception of Stage 2 of the cultural broker model—boundary spanning—was greatly influenced by this source.

Wright, D. J. (ed.). *Responding to the Needs of Today's Minority Students.* New Directions for Student Services, no. 38. San Francisco: Jossey-Bass, 1987.
This volume provides a valuable description of minority students and their needs on college campuses. Suggestions are made for creating a campus environment that is more hospitable to minority students.

References

Adler, J., and others. "Taking Offense: Is This the New Enlightenment on Campus or the New McCarthyism?" *Newsweek,* Dec. 24, 1990, pp. 48–54.

Altbach, P. G. "The Racial Dilemma in American Higher Education." In P. G. Altbach and K. Lomotey (eds.), *The Racial Crisis in American Higher Education.* Albany: State University of New York Press, 1991.

American Association of State Colleges and Universities. *Minorities in Public Higher Education: At a Turning Point.* Washington, D.C.: American Association of State Colleges and Universities, 1988.

American Council on Education. *The Student Personnel Point of View.* Washington, D.C.: American Council on Education, 1937.

American Council on Education. *The Student Personnel Point of View.* (Rev. ed.) Washington, D.C.: American Council on Education, 1949.

Anderson, J. "Cognitive Styles and Multicultural Populations." *Journal of Teacher Education,* 1988, *39* (1), 2–9.

Appleton, J. R., Briggs, C. M., and Rhatigan, J. J. *Pieces of Eight: The Rites, Roles, and Styles of the Dean by Eight Who Have Been There.* Portland, Oreg.: National Association of Student Personnel Administrators, 1978.

Argyris, C. "Theories of Action That Inhibit Individual Learning." *American Psychologist,* 1976, *33,* 638–654.

Aronowitz, S., and Giroux, H. *Postmodern Education.* Minneapolis: University of Minnesota Press, 1991.

Arredondo, P. "Counseling Latinas." In C. Lee and B. Richardson (eds.), *Multicultural Issues in Counseling.* Alexandria, Va.: American Association of Counseling and Development Media, 1991.

Astin, A. W. *Minorities in American Higher Education: Recent Trends, Current Prospects, and Recommendations.* San Francisco: Jossey-Bass, 1982.

Astin, A. W. *Achieving Educational Excellence: A Critical Assessment of Priorities and Practices in Higher Education.* San Francisco: Jossey-Bass, 1985.

Astin, A. W. "Excellence and Equity in the Education of Minority Students." Paper presented at the Minorities in Higher Education Conference, Hofstra University, Hempstead, New York, Mar. 1989.

Astone, B., and Nuñez-Wormack, E. *Pursuing Diversity: Recruiting College Minority Students.* ASHE-ERIC Higher Education Reports, no. 7. Washington, D.C.: Association for the Study of Higher Education, 1990.

Atkinson, D. R., Morten, G., and Sue, D. W. *Counseling American Minorities: A Cross-Cultural Perspective.* (3rd ed.) Dubuque, Iowa: Brown, 1989.

Banning, J. H. "Creating a Climate for Successful Student Development: The Campus Ecology Manager Role." In U. Delworth, G. R. Hanson, and Associates, *Student Services: A Handbook for the Profession.* (2nd ed.) San Francisco: Jossey-Bass, 1989.

Barker, R. *Ecological Psychology: Concepts for Studying the Environment of Human Behavior.* Stanford, Calif.: Stanford University Press, 1968.

Barr, D. J., and Strong, L. J. "Embracing Multiculturalism: The Existing Contradictions." *NASPA Journal,* 1988, *26* (2), 85–90.

Bennett, M. "A Developmental Approach to Training for Cultural Sensitivity." *International Journal of Intercultural Relations,* 1986, *10* (2), 179–196.

Bennett, W. J. *To Reclaim a Legacy.* Washington, D.C.: Study Group on the State of Learning in the Humanities in Higher Education, 1984.

Bennis, W. G. "The Coming Death of Bureaucracy." *Think,* Nov.–Dec. 1966, pp. 30–35.

Blake, J. H. "Approaching Minority Students as Assets." *Academe,* 1985, *71* (6), 19–21.

Bloland, P. "Leisure as a Campus Resource for Fostering Student Development." *Journal of Counseling and Development,* 1987, *65,* 291–294.

Bloom, A. *The Closing of the American Mind.* New York: Simon & Schuster, 1987.

Botstein, L. "The Undergraduate Curriculum and the Issue of Race." In P. Altbach and K. Lomotey (eds.), *The Racial Crisis in Higher Education.* Albany: State University of New York Press, 1991.

Brown, R. D. "Manipulation of the Environmental Press in a College Residence Hall." *Personnel and Guidance Journal,* 1968, *46,* 555–560.

Brown, R. D. "Fostering Intellectual and Personal Growth: The Student Development Role." In U. Delworth, G. R. Hanson, and Associates, *Student Services: A Handbook for the Profession.* (2nd ed.) San Francisco: Jossey-Bass, 1989.

Cass, V. "Homosexual Identity Formation: Testing a Theoretical Model." *Journal of Sex Research,* 1984, *20,* 143–167.

Chan, S., and Wang, L. "Racism and the Model Minority: Asian-Americans in Higher Education." In P. G. Altbach and K. Lomotey (eds.), *The Racial Crisis in Higher Education.* Albany: State University of New York Press, 1991.

Charbonneau, M., and John-Steiner, V. "Patterns of Experience and the Language of Mathematics." In R. Cocking and J. Mestre (eds.), *Linguistic and Cultural Influences on Learning Mathematics.* Hillsdale, N.J.: Erlbaum, 1988.

Chavez, E., and Carlson, J. "Building a Multicultural Campus Environment." *Bulletin of the Association of College Unions International,* 1986, *53* (5), 4–6.

Cheatham, H. E. "Affirming Affirmative Action." In H. E. Cheatham (ed.), *Cultural Pluralism on Campus.* Alexandria, Va.: American College Personnel Association Media, 1991a.

Cheatham, H. E. "Identity Development in a Pluralistic Society." In H. E. Cheatham (ed.), *Cultural Pluralism on Campus.* Alexandria, Va.: American College Personnel Association Media, 1991b.

Chickering, A. W. *Education and Identity.* San Francisco: Jossey-Bass, 1969.

Chisholm, S. "On Change." Keynote address at the annual meeting of the American College Personnel Association, Atlanta, Georgia, Mar. 1991.

Chung, R., and Okazaki, S. "Counseling Americans of Southeast Asian Descent." In C. C. Lee and B. L. Richardson (eds.), *Multicultural Issues in Counseling: New Approaches to Diversity.* Alexandria, Va.: American Association of Counseling and Development Media, 1991.

Cibik, M. A., and Chambers, S. L. "Similarities and Differences Among Native Americans, Hispanics, Blacks, and Anglos." *NASPA Journal,* 1991, *28* (2), 129–139.

Claney, D., and Parker, W. "Assessing White Racial Consciousness and Perceived Comfort with Black Individuals: A Preliminary Study." *Journal of Counseling and Development,* 1989, *67,* 449–451.

Cocking, R., and Mestre, J. "Considerations of Language Mediators of Mathematics Learning." In R. Cocking and J. Mestre (eds.), *Linguistic and Cultural Influences on Learning Mathematics.* Hillsdale, N.J.: Erlbaum, 1988.

Collison, M. N. "Racial Incidents Worry Campus Officials, University of Massachusetts Study." *Chronicle of Higher Education,* 1987, *33* (27), 1, 41.

Colon, A. "Race Relations on Campus: An Administrative Perspective." In P. G. Altbach and K. Lomotey (eds.), *The Racial Crisis in American Higher Education.* Albany: State University of New York Press, 1991.

Commission on Minority Participation in Education and American Life. *One Third of a Nation.* Washington, D.C.: American Council on Education and Education Commission of the States, 1988.

Cook, D., and Helms, J. "The Role of Counselors in Combating the 'New Racism' at Predominantly White Universities." In E. Herr and J. McFadden (eds.), *Challenges of Cultural and Racial Diversity to Counseling.* Alexandria, Va.: American Association of Counseling and Development Media, 1991.

Cross, K. P. *Adults as Learners: Increasing Participation and Facilitating Learning.* San Francisco: Jossey-Bass, 1981.

Cross, K. P. "Education for the 21st Century." *NASPA Journal,* 1985, *23* (1), 1–18.

Davenport, D., and Yurich, J. "Multicultural Gender Issues." *Journal of Counseling and Development,* 1991, *70* (1), 64–71.

DeCoster, D. "Effects of Homogeneous Housing Assignments for High Ability Students." *Journal of College Student Personnel,* 1968, *8,* 75–78.

DePalma, A. "Battling Bias, Campuses Face Free Speech Fight." *New York Times,* Feb. 20, 1991, p. B10.

Ebbers, L. H., and Henry, S. L. "Cultural Competence: A New Challenge to Student Affairs Professionals." *NASPA Journal,* 1990, *27* (4), 319–323.

Emerson, K. "Only Correct." *New Republic,* Feb. 1991, pp. 18–19.

Estrada, L. F. "Anticipating the Demographic Future: Dramatic Changes Are on the Way." *Change,* 1988, *20* (3), 14–19.

Evans, N. J., and Wall, V. A. *Beyond Tolerance: Gays, Lesbians, and Bisexuals on Campus.* Alexandria, Va.: American College Personnel Association Media, 1991.

Fellows, D. *A Mosaic of America's Ethnic Minorities.* New York: Wiley, 1972.

Fenske, R. H., and Hughes, M. S. "Current Challenges: Maintaining Quality Amid Increasing Student Diversity." In U. Delworth, G. R. Hanson, and Associates, *Student Services: A Handbook for the Profession.* (2nd ed.) San Francisco: Jossey-Bass, 1989.

Fields, C. "The Hispanic Pipeline: Narrow, Leaking, and Needing Repair." *Change,* 1988, *20* (3), 20–27.

Fleming, J. *Blacks in College: A Comparative Study of Students' Success in Black and White Institutions.* San Francisco: Jossey-Bass, 1984.

Freire, P. *Pedagogy of the Oppressed.* New York: Continuum, 1970.

Freire, P. *Education for Critical Consciousness.* New York: Continuum, 1973.

Freire, P. *The Politics of Education.* Boston: Bergin & Garvey, 1985.

Geertz, C. "The Uses of Diversity." *Michigan Quarterly Review,* 1986, *25* (1), 105–123.

Giddens, A. *Central Problems in Social Theory.* Berkeley and Los Angeles: University of California Press, 1979.

Giddens, A. *The Constitution of Society: Outline of the Theory of Structuration.* Los Angeles: University of California Press, 1984.

Gilligan, C. *In a Different Voice: Psychological Theory and Women's Development.* Cambridge, Mass.: Harvard University Press, 1982.

Giroux, H. A. "Border Pedagogy in the Age of Postmodernism." *Journal of Education,* 1988a, *170* (3), 162–181.

Giroux, H. A. *Schooling and the Struggle for Public Life.* Minneapolis: University of Minnesota Press, 1988b.

Gupta, N., and Manning, K. "Multiculturalism on Campus: Using Transformative Education to Understand." Paper presented at the annual meeting of the American College Personnel Association, San Francisco, Mar. 1992.

Haro, R. "Selecting a Dean of Student Services in the Far West: When Right May Be Wrong." *NASPA Journal,* 1991, *28* (2), 149–155.

Harris, S. M. "Evaluating University Programming for Minority Students." In H. E. Cheatham (ed.), *Cultural Pluralism on Campus.* Alexandria, Va.: American College Personnel Association Media, 1991.

Hayes, J. A. "Achieving Positive Race Relations: The Student Affairs Professional as a Risk Taker." *NASPA Journal,* 1985, *23* (1), 45–48.

Heath, S. B. *Ways with Words: Language, Life, and Work in Communities and Classrooms.* New York: Cambridge University Press, 1983.

Helgesen, S. *Women's Ways of Leading.* New York: Doubleday, 1990.

Helms, J. E. "Toward a Theoretical Explanation of the Effects of Race on Counseling: A Black and White Model." *Counseling Psychologist,* 1984, *12* (4), 153–164.

Helms, J. E. (ed.). *Black and White Racial Identity: Theory, Research, and Practice*. New York: Greenwood, 1991.

Higbee, J. L. "The Role of Developmental Education in Promoting Pluralism." In H. E. Cheatham (ed.), *Cultural Pluralism on Campus*. Alexandria, Va.: American College Personnel Association Media, 1991.

Hirsch, E. D., Jr. *Cultural Literacy: What Every American Needs to Know*. Boston: Houghton Mifflin, 1987.

Hodgkinson, H. L. *All One System: Demographics of Education, Kindergarten Through Graduate School*. Washington, D.C.: Institute for Educational Leadership, 1984.

Horowitz, H. L. "The 1960s and the Transformation of Campus Cultures." *History of Education Quarterly*, 1986, *26* (1), 1–38.

Hughes, M. S. "Black Students' Participation in Higher Education." *Journal of College Student Personnel*, 1987, *28*, 532–545.

Jackson, K. W. "Black Faculty in Academia." In P. G. Altbach and K. Lomotey (eds.), *The Racial Crisis in American Higher Education*. Albany: State University of New York Press, 1991.

Jacoby, B. "Today's Students: Diverse Needs Require Comprehensive Responses." In T. Miller, R. Winston, and Associates, *Administration and Leadership in Student Affairs: Actualizing Student Development in Higher Education*. Muncie, Ind.: Accelerated Development, 1991.

Jaschik, S. "Major Changes Seen Needed for Colleges to Attract Minorities." *Chronicle of Higher Education*, 1987, *34* (13), pp. 1, A31, A32.

Jones, A., Terrell, M., and Duggar, M. "The Role of Student Affairs in Fostering Cultural Diversity in Higher Education." *NASPA Journal*, 1991, *28* (2), 121–127.

Jones, J. "Racism in Black and White: A Bicultural Model of Reaction and Evolution." In P. Katz and D. Taylor (eds.), *Eliminating Racism: Profiles in Controversy*. New York: Plenum, 1988.

Jones, W. "Perspectives on Ethnicity." In L. V. Moore (ed.), *Evolving Theoretical Perspectives on Students*. New Directions for Student Services, no. 51. San Francisco: Jossey-Bass, 1990.

Katz, J. "The Sociopolitical Nature of Counseling." *Counseling Psychologist*, 1985, *13* (4), 615–624.

Katz, J. "The Challenge of Diversity." In C. Woolbright (ed.), *Valuing Diversity On Campus: A Multicultural Approach*. Bloomington, Ind.: Association of College Unions International, 1989.

Katz, P., and Taylor, D. *Eliminating Racism: Profiles in Controversy*. New York: Plenum Press, 1988.

Knefelkamp, L. "Developmental Instruction: Fostering Intellectual and Personal Growth of College Students." *Dissertation Abstracts International*, 1974, *36*, 1271A.

Kochman, T. *Black and White Styles in Conflict*. Chicago: University of Chicago Press, 1981.

Kohlberg, L. *Essays on Moral Development*. Vol. 2: *The Psychology of Moral Development*. New York: HarperCollins, 1984.

Kolb, D. *Learning Style Inventory: Self-Scoring Inventory and Interpretation Booklet*. Boston, Mass.: McBer, 1985.

Leafgren, F. (ed.). *Developing Campus Recreation and Wellness Programs*. New Directions for Student Services, no. 34. San Francisco: Jossey-Bass, 1986.

Leap, W. "Assumptions and Strategies Guiding Mathematics Problem Solving by Ute Indian Students." In R. Cocking and J. Mestre (eds.), *Linguistic and Cultural Influences on Learning Mathematics*. Hillsdale, N.J.: Erlbaum, 1988.

Lee, C., and Richardson, B. (eds.). *Multicultural Issues in Counseling: New Approaches to Diversity*. Alexandria, Va.: American Association of Counseling and Development Media, 1991.

Leifer, A. "Ethnic Patterns in Cognitive Tasks." *Proceedings of the Annual Convention of the American Psychological Association*, 1972, *7*, 73–74.

Leppo, J. "Multicultural Programming: A Conceptual Framework and Model for Implementation." *Campus Activities Programming*, 1987, *10* (9), 56–60.

Lesser, G. S., Fifer, G., and Clark, D. H. "Mental Abilities of Children from Different Social Class and Cultural Groups." Monographs for the Society of Research in Child Development, 1965, *30* (4, serial no. 30).

Lloyd-Jones, E. "Foreword." In D. Roberts (ed.), *Designing Campus Activities to Foster a Sense of Community*. New Directions for Student Services, no. 48. San Francisco: Jossey-Bass, 1989.

Locust, D. "Wounding the Spirit: Discrimination and Traditional American Indian Belief Systems." *Harvard Educational Review*, 1988, *58* (3), 315–330.

McEwen, M. K., Roper, L. D., Bryant, D. R., and Langa, M. J. "Incorporating the Development of African-American Students into Psychosocial Theories of Student Development." *Journal of College Student Development*, 1990, *31* (5), 429–436.

Mackenzie, G. "Fallacies of PC." *Chronicle of Higher Education*, 1991, *38* (2), pp. B1–B2.

Mangrum, C., and Strichart, S. *College and the Learning Disabled Student*. Philadelphia: Grune & Stratton, 1984.

Manning, K. *Ways with Words in Colleges*. Unpublished manuscript, Indiana University, 1987.

Manning, K. "The Multi-Cultural Challenge of the 1990s." *Campus Activities Programming*, 1988, *21* (4), 53–56.

Manning, K. "Campus Ritual and Cultural Meaning." Unpublished doctoral dissertation, Educational Leadership and Policy Studies, Indiana University, 1989.

Manning, K. "The Case Study." In F. K. Stage (ed.), *Diverse Methods for Research and Assessment of College Students*. Alexandria, Va.: American College Personnel Association Media, 1992.

Manning, K., and Coleman-Boatwright, P. "Student Affairs Initiatives Toward a Multicultural University." *Journal of College Student Development*, 1991, *32* (4), 367–374.

Manning, K., and Stage, F. K. "Personalizing the College Context from a Cultural Perspective." Paper presented at the annual meeting of the National Association for Student Personnel Administrators, St. Louis, Missouri, Mar. 1987.

Marin, P. "The Methods of Protest of a Latina: Culturally and Historically Bound." Unpublished manuscript, University of Vermont, 1992.

Mentkowski, M., and Doherty, A. "Abilities That Last a Lifetime: Outcomes of the Alverno Experience." *American Association for Higher Education Bulletin*, 1984, *36*, 5–6, 11–14.

Milne, N. "The Experiences of College Students with Learning Disabilities." Unpublished doctoral dissertation, Educational Leadership and Policy Studies, Indiana University, 1989.

Miser, K. (ed.). *Student Affairs and Campus Dissent: Reflection of the Past and Challenge of the Future*. NASPA Monograph Series, no. 8. Washington, D.C.: National Association of Student Personnel Administrators, 1988.

Moore, L. V. (ed.). *Evolving Theoretical Perspectives on Students*. New Directions for Student Services, no. 51. San Francisco: Jossey-Bass, 1990.

Moore, M., and Delworth, U. *Training Manual for Student Service Program Development*. Boulder, Colo.: Western Interstate Commission for Higher Education, 1976.

Morrill, W. H. "Program Development." In U. Delworth, G. R. Hanson, and Associates, *Student Services: A Handbook for the Profession*. (2nd ed.) San Francisco: Jossey-Bass, 1989.

Munoz, D. G. "Identifying Areas of Stress for Chicano Undergraduates." In M. A. Olivas (ed.), *Latino College Students*. New York: Teachers College Press, 1986.

Nora, A., and Rendon, L. "Determinants of Predisposition to Transfer Among Community College Students: A Structural Model." *Research in Higher Education*, 1990, *31* (3), 235–255.

Olivas, M. A. (ed.). "Research on Latino College Students: A Theoretical Framework and Inquiry." In M. A. Olivas (ed.), *Latino College Students*. New York: Teachers College Press, 1986.

Orasanu, J., Lee, C., and Scribner, S. "Free Recall: Ethnic and Economic Group." *Child Development*, 1979, *50*, 1100–1109.

Pace, C. *Measuring Outcomes of College: Fifty Years of Findings and Recommendations for the Future*. San Francisco: Jossey-Bass, 1979.

Pace, C. *Measuring the Quality of College Student Experiences*. Los Angeles: Higher Education Research Institute, University of California, 1988.

Palafox, N., and Warren, A. *Cross-Cultural Caring*. Honolulu: John A. Burns School of Medicine, University of Hawaii, 1980.

Pascarella, E. T. "Students' Affective Development Within the College Environment." *Journal of Higher Education*, 1985, *56*, 640–663.

Pascarella, E. T., and Terenzini, P. T. *How College Affects Students: Findings and Insights from Twenty Years of Research*. San Francisco: Jossey-Bass, 1991.

Perry, W. *Forms of Intellectual and Ethical Development in the College Years: A Scheme*. Troy, Mo.: Holt, Rinehart & Winston, 1970.

Phelps, R. E., Meara, N. M., Davis, K. L., and Patton, M. J. "Blacks' and Whites' Perceptions of Verbal Aggression." *Journal of Counseling and Development*, 1991, *69*, 345–350.

Pounds, A. W. "Black Students' Needs on Predominantly White Campuses." In D. J. Wright (ed.), *Responding to the Needs of Today's Minority Students*. New Directions for Student Services, no. 38. San Francisco: Jossey-Bass, 1987.

Powell, B., and Steelman, L. C. "Variations in State SAT Performance: Meaningful or Misleading?" *Harvard Educational Review*, 1984, *54* (4), 389–412.

Richardson, R. C., Simmons, H., and de los Santos, A. "Graduating Minority Students: Lessons from Ten Success Stories." *Change*, 1987, *19* (3), 20–27.

Richardson, R. C., and Skinner, E. F. "Adapting to Diversity: Organizational Influences on Student Achievement." *Journal of Higher Education*, 1990, *61* (5), 485–511.

Ringgenberg, L. "Expanding Participation of Student Subgroups in Campus Activities." In D. Roberts (ed.), *Designing Campus Activities to Foster a Sense of Community*. New Directions for Student Services, no. 48. San Francisco: Jossey-Bass, 1989.

Rothschadl, A. M., and Russell, R. V. "Improving Teaching Effectiveness: Addressing Modes of Learning in the College Classroom." *Schole: A Journal of Recreation Education and Leisure Studies*, 1992, 7.

Russell, R. *Planning Programs in Recreation*. St. Louis, Mo.: Times Mirror/Mosby, 1982.

Russell, R. V., and Rothschadl, A. M. "Learning Styles: Another View of the College Classroom?" *Schole: A Journal of Recreation Education and Leisure Studies*, 1991, 6.

Sagaria, M.A.D. (ed.). *Empowering Women: Leadership Development Strategies on Campus*. New Directions for Student Services, no. 44. San Francisco: Jossey-Bass, 1988.

Schaef, A. *Women's Reality*. Minneapolis, Minn.: Winston, 1985.

Schlossberg, N. "Marginality and Mattering: Key Issues in Building Community." In D. C. Roberts (ed.), *Designing Campus Activities to Foster a Sense of Community*. New Directions for Student Services, no. 48. San Francisco: Jossey-Bass, 1989.

Sears, D. "Symbolic Racism." In P. Katz and D. Taylor (eds.), *Eliminating Racism*. New York: Plenum Press, 1988.

Sedlacek, W. "Black Students on White Campuses: Twenty Years of Research." *Journal of College Student Personnel*, 1987, *28* (6), 484–495.

Shade, B. J. "African-American Cognitive Style: A Variable in School Success?" *Review of Educational Research*, 1982, *52* (2), 219–244.

Sigel, I. E., Anderson, L. M., and Shapiro, H. "Perceptual Categorization of Lower and Middle Class Negro School Children." *Journal of Negro Education*, 1966, *35*, 218–229.

Siggelkow, R. A. "Racism in Higher Education: A Permanent Condition?" *NASPA Journal*, 1991, *28* (2), 98–104.

Simonson, R., and Walker, S. *The Graywolf Annual Five: Multicultural Literacy, Opening the American Mind*. St. Paul, Minn.: Graywolf Press, 1988.

Smith, D. *The Challenge of Diversity: Involvement or Alienation in the Academy?* ASHE/ERIC Higher Education Reports, no. 5. Washington, D.C.: Association for the Study of Higher Education, 1989.

Smith, P. *Killing the Spirit*. New York: Viking Penguin, 1990.

Solomon, L. C., and Wingard, T. L. "The Changing Demographics: Problems and Opportunities." In P. G. Altbach and K. Lomotey (eds.), *The Racial Crisis in American Higher Education*. Albany: State University of New York Press, 1991.

Stage, F. K. "College Outcomes and Student Development: Filling the Gaps." *Review of Higher Education,* 1989a, *12* (3), 293–304.

Stage, F. K. "Motivation, Academic and Social Integration, and the Early Dropout." *American Educational Research Journal,* 1989b, *26* (3), 385–402.

Stage, F. K. "Research on College Students: Commonality, Difference, and Direction." *Review of Higher Education,* 1990, *13* (3), 249–258.

Stage, F. K. "The Case for Flexibility in Assessing and Conducting Research on College Students." In F. K. Stage (ed.), *Diverse Methods for Assessing and Conducting Research on College Students.* Alexandria, Va.: American College Personnel Association Media, 1992a.

Stage, F. K. (ed.). *Diverse Methods for Assessing and Conducting Research on College Students.* Alexandria, Va.: American College Personnel Association Media, 1992b.

Stage, F. K., Schuh, J. H., Hosler, D., and Westfall, S. B. "Residence Hall Staff Use of Student Development Theory: Differences by Experience and Educational Level." *NASPA Journal,* 1991, *28* (4), 292–297.

Steele, S. "The Recoloring of Campus Life: Student Racism, Academic Pluralism, and the End of a Dream." *Harper's,* Feb. 1989, pp. 47–55.

Steele, S. *The Content of Our Character.* New York: St. Martin's, 1990.

Stodolsky, S., and Lesser, G. "Learning Patterns in the Disadvantaged." *Harvard Educational Review,* 1967, *37,* 546–593.

Strong, L. "Multiculturalism as a Management Style: Toward a New Method of Supervision." George Washington University, Washington, D.C., unpublished manuscript, 1988.

Sue, D., and Sue, D. W. "Counseling Strategies for Chinese Americans." In C. Lee and B. Richardson (eds.), *Multicultural Issues in Counseling: New Approaches to Diversity.* Alexandria, Va.: American Association of Counseling and Development Media, 1991.

Sue, D. W. "The Challenge of Multiculturalism: The Road Less Traveled." *American Counselor,* 1992, *1* (1), 6–14.

Sue, D. W., and Sue, D. "Chinese-American Personality and Mental Health." *Amerasia Journal,* 1985, *1,* 36–49.

Sue, D. W., and Sue, D. *Counseling the Culturally Different: Theory and Practice.* (2nd ed.) New York: Wiley, 1990.

Suina, J. "Epilogue: 'And Then I Went to School.' " In R. Cocking and J. Mestre (eds.), *Linguistic and Cultural Influences on Learning Mathematics.* Hillsdale, N.J.: Erlbaum, 1988.

Taylor, C. A. "Black Students on Predominantly White College Campuses in the 1980s." *Journal of College Student Personnel,* 1986, *27,* 196–201.

Taylor, J. "Are You Politically Correct?" *New York Magazine,* Jan. 1991, pp. 33–40.

Thiers, N. "Education Report on Black Students Disputed." *Guideposts,* 1987, *30* (6), 1, 6.

Tierney, W. G. "The College Experience of Native Americans: A Critical Analysis." In L. Weis and M. Fine (eds.), *Silenced Voices: Issues of Class, Race, and Gender in Today's Schools.* New York: State University of New York Press, 1991.

Tinto, V. "Dropout from Higher Education: A Theoretical Synthesis of Recent Research." *Review of Educational Research,* 1975, *45,* 89–125.

Tomine, S. "Counseling Japanese Americans: From Internment to Reparation." In C. Lee and B. Richardson (eds.), *Multicultural Issues in Counseling: New Approaches to Diversity.* Alexandria, Va.: American Association of Counseling and Development Media, 1991.

VanBebber, L. "Integrating Diversity into Traditional Resident Assistant Courses." In H. E. Cheatham (ed.), *Cultural Pluralism on Campus.* Alexandria, Va.: American College Personnel Association Media, 1991.

Weinrach, S. G. "Microcounseling and Beyond: A Dialogue with Allen Ivey." *Journal of Counseling and Development,* 1987, *65,* 532–537.

Wilson, R., and Carter, D. J. *Minorities in Higher Education: Seventh Annual Status Report.* Washington, D.C.: American Council on Education, 1988.

Winston, R., and Ender, S. "Use of Student Paraprofessionals in Divisions of College Student Affairs." *Journal of Counseling and Development,* 1988, *66* (10), 466–473.

Wright, D. J. (ed.). *Responding to the Needs of Today's Minority Students*. New Directions for Student Services, no. 38. San Francisco: Jossey-Bass, 1987.

Zeller, W., Hinni, J., and Eison, J. "Creating Educational Partnerships Between Academic and Student Affairs." In D. Roberts (ed.), *Designing Campus Activities to Foster a Sense of Community*. New Directions for Student Services, no. 48. San Francisco: Jossey-Bass, 1989.

INDEX

Academics: and classroom materials, 38–
39; and diversity, 37–38; and infor-
mation processing, 39–40; vignette
on, 5, 7, 41, 44–45
Action. *See* Taking action
Activities. *See* Cocurriculum
Adler, J., 10, 31
Administrators, student affairs, 2; and
academic environment, 45; and cul-
tural broker model, 25–35; as cul-
tural brokers, 41–42
Advisory committees, 28–29
Affirmative action, 31, 32
African Americans. *See* Multicultural
students
Altbach, P. G., 28, 48, 51, 75
Alverno College, 65
American Association of State Colleges
and Universities, 8, 9, 12
American Council on Education, 52–53
Anderson, J., 37, 40, 43
Anderson, L. M., 39
Appleton, J. R., 53
Argyris, C., 14
Aronowitz, S., 27, 48, 51, 52
Arredondo, P., 30, 52
Astin, A. W., 18, 20, 33, 65
Astone, B., 25, 48, 49, 52
Atkinson, D. R., 18, 20, 34, 47, 50, 51,
59, 60, 61, 75
Authority, and equity, 26–27

Banning, J. H., 58
Barker, R., 37
Barr, D. J., 34
Barriers, removing, and multicultural
approach, 34
Bennett, C., 38
Bennett, M., 59
Bennett, W. J., 27, 51
Bennis, W. G., 25
Blake, J. H., 9, 18, 43
Bloland, P., 65
Bloom, A., 9, 27, 51
Border-crossers, 14, 74–75
Botstein, L., 20, 27, 29, 52
Briggs, C. M., 53

Brown, R. D., 41, 57, 58
Bryant, D. R., 10, 21

Campus: diverse, 67–69; as hostile en-
vironment, 47–49; monocultural, 3,
15–16, 26. *See also* Multicultural cam-
pus
Carlson, J., 66
Carter, D. J., 9, 12
Cass, V., 59
Chambers, S. L., 21
Chan, S., 48
Charbonneau, M., 40
Chavez, E., 66
Cheatham, H. E., 10, 75
Chickering, A. W., 22, 53
Chisholm, S., 10
Chung, R., 49
Cibik, M. A., 21
Claney, D., 33, 47, 50
Clark, D. H., 39
Classroom: materials for, 38–39; style
of, 37–38
Cocking, R., 40
Cocurriculum, 65–66; on diverse cam-
pus, 67–69; events of, 29; vignette
about, 5–6, 7, 44–45
Coleman-Boatwright, P., 9, 20, 30, 31,
33, 47, 61
Collison, M. N., 9
Colon, A., 15, 34, 47, 51
Commission on Minority Participation
in Education and American Life, 8, 9,
12
Communication: cross-cultural, 30–31;
with students, 54–55
Conflict management, with multi-
culturalism, 31
Contextualism. *See* Thinking contextu-
ally
Cook, D., 20, 21, 26, 27, 47, 48, 50
Counseling, cross-cultural, 51–52. *See
also* Cultural broker; Student advocacy
Cross, K. P., 9, 67
Cultural broker model, 2, 16–23; and
academics, 37–45; and administra-

89

ORDERING INFORMATION

NEW DIRECTIONS FOR STUDENT SERVICES is a series of paperback books that offers guidelines and programs for aiding students in their total development—emotional, social, and physical, as well as intellectual. Books in the series are published quarterly in Spring, Summer, Fall, and Winter, and are available for purchase by subscription as well as by single copy.

SUBSCRIPTIONS for 1992 cost $45.00 for individuals (a savings of 20 percent over single-copy prices) and $60.00 for institutions, agencies, and libraries. Please do not send institutional checks for personal subscriptions. Standing orders are accepted.

SINGLE COPIES cost $14.95 when payment accompanies order. (California, New Jersey, New York, and Washington, D.C., residents please include appropriate sales tax.) Billed orders will be charged postage and handling.

DISCOUNTS for quantity orders are available. Please write to the address below for information.

ALL ORDERS must include either the name of an individual or an official purchase order number. Please submit your order as follows:
 Subscriptions: specify series and year subscription is to begin
 Single copies: include individual title code (such as SS1)

MAIL ALL ORDERS TO:
 Jossey-Bass Publishers
 350 Sansome Street
 San Francisco, California 94104

FOR SALES OUTSIDE OF THE UNITED STATES CONTACT:
 Maxwell Macmillan International Publishing Group
 866 Third Avenue
 New York, New York 10022

OTHER TITLES AVAILABLE IN THE
NEW DIRECTIONS FOR STUDENT SERVICES SERIES
Margaret J. Barr, Editor-in-Chief
M. Lee Upcraft, Associate Editor

U.S. Postal Service

STATEMENT OF OWNERSHIP, MANAGEMENT AND CIRCULATION
Required by 39 U.S.C. 3685)

1A. Title of Publication	1B. PUBLICATION NO.	2. Date of Filing
NEW DIRECTIONS FOR STUDENT SERVICES	4 4 9 – 0 7 0	10/16/92

3. Frequency of Issue	3A. No. of Issues Published Annually	3B. Annual Subscription Price
Quarterly	Four (4)	$45(individual) $60(institutional)

4. Complete Mailing Address of Known Office of Publication *(Street, City, County, State and ZIP+4 Code) (Not printers)*

350 Sansome Street, San Francisco, CA 94104-1310

5. Complete Mailing Address of the Headquarters of General Business Offices of the Publisher *(Not printer)*

Same as above.

6. Full Names and Complete Mailing Address of Publisher, Editor, and Managing Editor *(This item MUST NOT be blank)*

Publisher *(Name and Complete Mailing Address)*

Jossey-Bass Inc., Publishers (same address as 4 above.)

Editor *(Name and Complete Mailing Address)*
Margaret J. Barr, 633 Clark Street, 2-219, Evanston, IL 60208-1103

Managing Editor *(Name and Complete Mailing Address)*

Lynn Luckow, President, Jossey-Bass Inc., Publishers

7. Owner *(If owned by a corporation, its name and address must be stated and also immediately thereunder the names and addresses of stockholders owning or holding 1 percent or more of total amount of stock. If not owned by a corporation, the names and addresses of the individual owners must be given. If owned by a partnership or other unincorporated firm, its name and address, as well as that of each individual must be given. If the publication is published by a nonprofit organization, its name and address must be stated.) (Item must be completed.)*

Full Name	Complete Mailing Address
Maxwell Communications Corp., plc	Headington Hill Hall Oxford OX30BW U.K.

8. Known Bondholders, Mortgagees, and Other Security Holders Owning or Holding 1 Percent or More of Total Amount of Bonds, Mortgages or Other Securities *(If there are none, so state)*

Full Name	Complete Mailing Address
Same as 7 above.	Same as 7 above.

9. For Completion by Nonprofit Organizations Authorized To Mail at Special Rates *(DMM Section 423.12 only)*
The purpose, function, and nonprofit status of this organization and the exempt status for Federal income tax purposes *(Check one)*

(1) ☐ Has Not Changed During Preceding 12 Months	(2) ☐ Has Changed During Preceding 12 Months	*(If changed, publisher must submit explanation of change with this statement.)*

10.	Extent and Nature of Circulation *(See instructions on reverse side)*	Average No. Copies Each Issue During Preceding 12 Months	Actual No. Copies of Single Issue Published Nearest to Filing Date
A.	Total No. Copies *(Net Press Run)*	2100	2226
B.	Paid and/or Requested Circulation 1. Sales through dealers and carriers, street vendors and counter sales	164	122
	2. Mail Subscription *(Paid and/or requested)*	1021	1062
C.	Total Paid and/or Requested Circulation *(Sum of 10B1 and 10B2)*	1185	1184
D.	Free Distribution by Mail, Carrier or Other Means Samples, Complimentary, and Other Free Copies	52	145
E.	Total Distribution *(Sum of C and D)*	1237	1329
F.	Copies Not Distributed 1. Office use, left over, unaccounted, spoiled after printing	863	897
	2. Return from News Agents	-0-	-0-
G.	TOTAL *(Sum of E, F1 and 2—should equal net press run shown in A)*	2100	2226

11. I certify that the statements made by me above are correct and complete	Signature and Title of Editor, Publisher, Business Manager, or Owner *Larry Ishii* Larry Ishii Vice-President

PS Form 3526, Feb. 1989 *(See instructions on reverse)*